CHANGE YOUR MINDSET

THROUGH

The Eight Fundamental Principles Of Creation

Through Your Manifestation

Of

Animated Geomancy

Via

Meditation

To Access Your Eternal Light Body

BY
LoveLifeLee

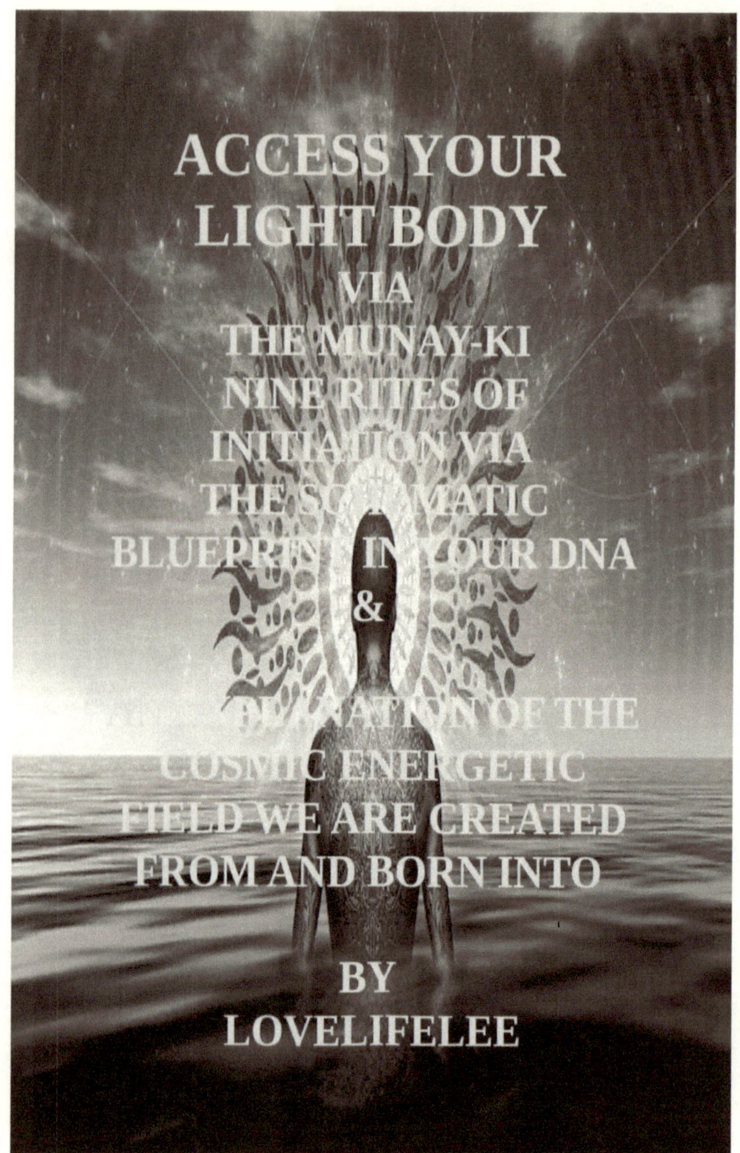
ACCESS YOUR
LIGHT BODY
VIA
THE MUNAY-KI
NINE RITES OF
INITIATION VIA
THE SOMATIC
BLUEPRINT IN YOUR DNA
&
ACTIVATION OF THE
COSMIC ENERGETIC
FIELD WE ARE CREATED
FROM AND BORN INTO

BY
LOVELIFELEE

MEDITATION
THE KEY TO
PEACEFUL
MANIFESTATION
ALLOWING ACCESS
TO YOUR
LIGHTBODY
BY
LOVE LIFE LEE

A Star Seeds Perception Of The Creation & The Science Of Evolution

Learn How To Fully Activate Your Pineal Gland Chakra Light Filament Antennas To Activate The Light Sphere Halo Around Your Head

To Move From Being In The Mind Back Into Your Heart Space

So That Your Light Sphere Halo Can Be Connected To Your Merkaba Light Body Field

& A Star Seeds Deciphering Of Information & Consciousness Awakening On Earth & Their Psychic Connection To Their Star Families

With Knowledge Of Your DNA & The Biological Make Up Of Your Eternal Divine Angelic Human Avatar

BY
LoveLifeLee

PAGE INDEX AT BACK OF BOOK

https://www.feedaread.com/search/books.aspx?keywords=Love%20life%20Lee
FEEDAREAD.COM
Book Search

Published in 2023 by FeedARead.com Publishing

A CIP catalogue record for this title is available from the British Library.

Other Books By Love Life Lee

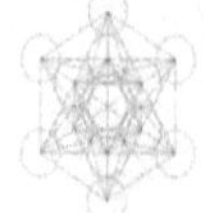 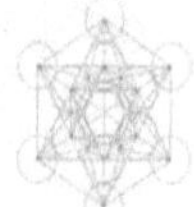

THE
SCAFFOLDING OF LIFE

**The Wonderful World Of
Geometric Matter
The Building Blocks
Of All Biological Life &
Our Universe
Access The Blueprint In
Your DNA
Grow A Rainbow Light Body
Stop Karmic Cycles & Evolve
Transcend Time & Space &
Ascension You Will Achieve
BY
LOVE LIFE LEE**

The Scaffolding Of Life
The Building Blocks Of Sacred Geometry
Learn The Secrets Of Our Physical Universe &
Biological Makeup Of Our DNA, How To Evolve
Consciously Transcend Time & Space
To Learn How To Transverse The Universe With
Thought Mind Body & Spirit
Using Your Conscious Energy
Using Your Life Force Understand Your Full
Potential Grow A New Body Into Being
Consciously Evolve & Ascend
Create A Rainbow Body Of Light
Your Divine Right

Other Books By Love Life Lee

THE PASSAGE
OF
ASCENSION
ACTIVATE YOUR
LIGHT BODY

At the Eckatic level of full expanded
Consciousness, Knowledge of the
Keys to Activation from the Yanas
the Ascended Masters of the First
Primal Sound Field, the Eternal
Yunasai Source Collective
Consciousness that formed the
Three Primal Sound Fields of the
Khundaray Hyper-Dimensional
Holographical Light Energy Time
Matrix of Creation known as
Geomancy

BY
LOVE LIFE LEE

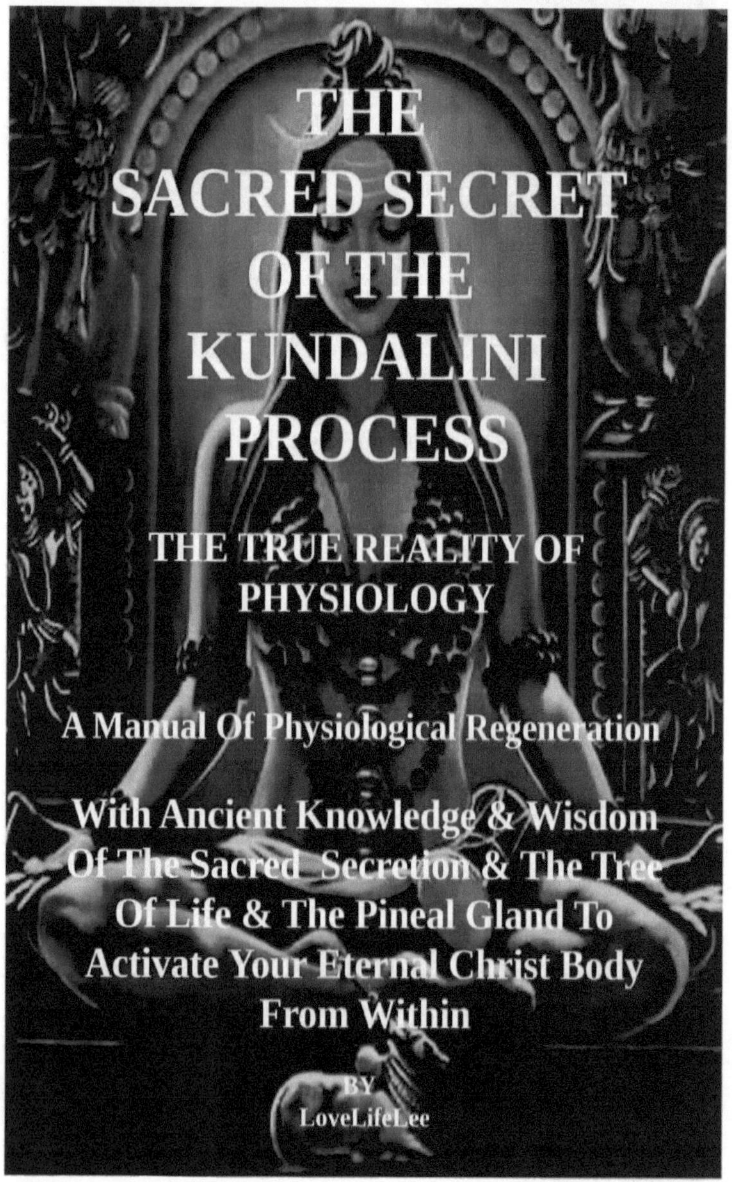
THE
SACRED SECRET
OF THE
KUNDALINI
PROCESS

THE TRUE REALITY OF
PHYSIOLOGY

A Manual Of Physiological Regeneration

With Ancient Knowledge & Wisdom
Of The Sacred Secretion & The Tree
Of Life & The Pineal Gland To
Activate Your Eternal Christ Body
From Within

BY
LoveLifeLee

CHAPTER ONE

A Star Seeds Deciphering Of Information & Consciousness Awakening On Planet Gaia

One day I realized that all the study I had done in my life time up to that point had raised my Consciousness from decades of critical thinking that I had used to critically research information on this Planet Gaia. It had been an extreme challenge processing all the data I had collected, and a challenge learning to decipher between the lies, manipulation, and deception of information I was collecting and processing. I learnt that eighty five percent of the information was misinformation to deceive, manipulate, and push humanity down a negative timeline, where humanity would not be in control of their own destiny of manifestation towards their positive timeline to evolve into their Mer-Ka-Ba fields of light. So that humanity could access their eternal human light body, to stop the karmic cycles of life and death via accessing their full twelve strands of DNA. So that humanity could ascend and move freely at will within the Holographical Hyperdimensional Light Time Templar Matrix, and beyond in the true reality outside of this Holographical Hyperdimensional Light Time Templar Matrix, in the Eternal realms, that's all created through all the light spectrums resonating at different vibrational frequencies. I realized that many negative spirits and extraterrestrials in many different physical avatar forms of energy were manipulating humanity from the ether dimensions, from different realms in the etheric planes. I also realized that these negative spirits and races and their collectives were trying to control humanity via their DNA gene pools, to manipulate humanity to take a negative timeline to take control of humanities collective consciousness. To control the human race and to control the Planet, and to manipulate humanity to believe that when they are contacted by these negative beings and their collectives, when they manifest in humans dreams, or via psychic contact interaction, or via physical manifestation in their physical avatar forms in face to face contact and interactions, that their intentions are to help humanity, but it appears this is not the case, that they have their own agenda's that benefit their own species.

I also came to the realization that we have manifested into all or most of the different species of this Universe to experience their perspective of life and the Creation from their view point, over eons and eons. I also became conscious that I had left the eternal realms leaving the energetic Ultra Violet Plasma Source Consciousness field, leaving as a single cell of the Source field collective in my natural state of ultra violet Source plasma consciousness energy weighing twenty one grams, to manifest as an Ascended Master in the highest dimension. I also recognized that I have manifested as a blue skinned being over thirty feet tall, I also recognized that I had manifested in the fifth, sixth, and seventh dimension into extraterrestrial races living thousands of years. I also recognized that I chose to leave my extraterrestrial family and friends for a twenty six thousand year cycle of manifestation in human form on the Planet Gaia for a mission and for a human three dimensional physical experience for Spiritual growth. My wish was to manifest on the Planet Gaia and learn ancient knowledge to raise my consciousness so I could attain the knowledge and wisdom to teach humanity about their Mer-Ka-Ba field, their eternal human light body. Which is accessed via their conscious awareness focused on their twelve strands of DNA with intentional manifestation, so that they can escape the Mind and the Holographical Hyperdimensional Light Time Templar Matrix, that is the encompassing illusion of reality. I also came to Planet Gaia to access my own eternal human light body via the Mer-Ka-Ba field to evolve and ascend, to transcend to help in the ascension process of the human race on the Planet from the third dimension to the fifth dimension of consciousness, to help in the evolution of this human race. I chose to come to Planet Gaia so that the manipulation and interference cycles by negative spirits, entities, species and their collective forces of the negative polarity, could be broken and stopped, after thousand years of genetic manipulation, especially the last thirteen thousand years. So that humanity could be freed to evolve and choose their own positive future directed timeline by evolving into an eternal human race and entering the eternal realms, where they have many different species as eternal allies. That will unite with them in this great eternal Spiritual interdimensional Genetic Seed War, that has been raging on for billions and billions of years, because this Genetic Seed War has been going on for eons and eons, between the Christos Collectives and the Fallen Angel races.

So when we manifest from our higher dimensional Planet onto another lower dimensional Planet, we are doing this through the Interdimensional Association of Free Worlds, that has many species members of the Christos Collectives. Which is a huge gigantic organization of Christos Collectives of positive species with over twenty four billion members from various different Interdimensional races and Interstellar World Nations. When we are leaving higher dimensions to manifest in lower dimensions like on Planet Gaia, its through the Interdimensional Association of Free Worlds, we are doing this through the Emerald Covenant agreement. We manifest and fight Spiritually, psychically, and physically against the Fallen Angel Collectives in their various energetic forms and physical extraterrestrial race forms, to stop these negative races that want to dominate, enslave, and exterminate the Christos Collectives races from this Universe. So we manifest in this lower dimensional Genetic Seed War to help other suppressed races and to bring balance to the Creation.

So the Oraphim Angelic Human Indigo bloodline lineages are super advanced genetic Eternal Divine Light beings that are extremely sophisticated. But over time with the concealment of ancient Cosmic knowledge and wisdom, and with the genetic manipulation of our DNA, including the manipulation of mind control

through Artificial Intelligence and other technologies, and via toxic chemicals, the human races have become sedated and have been living there lifes walking about in a dream state in an illusion of reality, disconnected from Spirit, from the Universal Ether of the Zero Point Energy field of the Holographical HyperDimensional Light Time Templar Matrix of Creation. The human race have also been disconnected by the fractal distortions in the Planet's electromagnetic grids, this severed and cut off our connection to our own DNA Schematic Blueprint Template, that can upgrade our DNA to grow a new body that lives differently, dies differently, and heals differently.
The Creators of this entire Hyperdimensional Light Time Templar Matrix, the Yanas Consciousness Collective and their Three Founder races have been passing this knowledge onto all species of races

for around Nine Hundred and Forty Nine billion years, and it has been passed onto the Oraphim Human Lineage for around Five Hundred and Seventy Nine million years, when the first original Angelic Human Schematic Blueprint was created.

So when we have clarity and access the higher levels of Consciousness we can arrive at the understanding of the multidimensional reality of our biological energetic avatar structure. It is actually the Lower Density aspects of our Higher Selves that reside in the distinct higher Dimensions of Creation and beyond in the Spirit realms. We then come to realize that we are the Ones we have been waiting for, we are the Yanas, the Eieyani, the Elohei Elohim Breneau, the Founder Races, we are the Guardians, the Keepers of the past, present, and future. We are the Caretakers of the Light Time Templar Matrix manifesting in these lower densities to make change from within the human race on Planet Gaia.

Our higher selves of the Blue, Gold, and Violet Energetic Consciousness Collectives perceive us as bredwin, it is with their true nature of understanding and knowing of the magnitude of challenges, and the difficulties we face in this lower dimension while descending on a mission on behalf of the Oneness Source Collective. So this is why they have compassion for us as we wake up to our higher Collectives, and the ancient knowledge and wisdom of healing ourselves and that of the Planets electromagnetic fields, via accessing our fully activated twelve strands of DNA.

Long ago in our Universal history around Nine Hundred and Forty Nine billion years ago the ancient Eternal Founder races of this Universe initially provided knowledge of the Emerald Covernant wisdom to their genetically created races and to the races that they genetically created, knowledge that was there Intrinsic heritage, as it is for all Spiritual beings, its their Universal

Eternal birth right. This wisdom comes from the three Founding Original Founder races known as the Emerald Order Breneau, that are the Feline Hominid - Anuhazi Feline Elohim race, the Cetacean Aquatic Ape Pegasus - Pegasai race and the Avian Insect Reptile – Cerez race. Their Melchizedek Cloister Emerald Order lessons of knowledge of our Universal Light Time Matrix Life field evolved from the ancient eternal Founder races, it is the legacy of the Source Creation of the Three Primal Sound Fields emmited from Source, the Blue, Gold, and Violet Light Consciousness fields, that created this Super Advanced Biological Holographical Light Density DNA Technology, that is living and animated vigorously by Spirit, the Eternal essence of Source. These Cosmic teachings of Spiritual growth enabling DNA upgrading to ascend beyond the Holographical Matrix, were common knowledge in our past Planetary history over thirteen thousand years ago, and going back in the Universe around Nine Hundred and Forty Nine billion years ago. The societies living on Planet Earth before thirteen thousand years ago were of Christos Consciousness philosophy of the Law of One mind sets, with a Love based peaceful enlightened Angelic Human civilization all unified as a cohesive Collective, that were on the verge of becoming an Eternal Super Human race. The Lyran Human Divine Blueprint bloodlines known as the (The Lighted Ones) of the Oraphim Angelic Human race which are the Eieyani Intrinsic Essence Grail bloodlines, and we are also known as the Turaneusiam Human race meaning the (Children of the Lighted Ones), they were created specifically so the ancient Emerald Breneau Founder races Collective could incarnate into the bloodlines of the Lyran Sirian bloodlines and the Earth's Indigo children bloodlines. So that they could be used by the Christos Collective to manifest directly down the Dimensions into Third, Fourth, and Fifth Density, and incarnate for emergency intervention to effect change from within the human species directly, by raising frequencies and Consciousness and to connect the Twelve strands of DNA of the Human Avatar to access its full potential to open humanities Light Body's. Allowing humanity to evolve, to use our DNA activated Light Body to repair the fractal fragmented electromagnetic fields of the Planet, and the fabric of the DNA Creation Fields, and to also then metamorphosis into the Cosmic Eternal Human race, that's no longer able to then be controlled or manipulated by negative Service to Self races.

The Law of One pilosophies are the teachings of the Christos Founder races from the Melchizedek Cloister Emerald Order, this wisdom of knowledge allows Eternal Spirit Souls manifesting in different races to upgrade there Consciousness and

DNA, allowing them to evolve to eventually become part of the Eternal Cosmic family of Light, living fully embodied but able to transverse inside time and space in the Holographical Hyperdimensional Matrix of the living Light DNA simulation, and to reside in the Eternal realms outside time and space in the Kingdom of Lights Spiritual realms. The wisdom they pass on is of the inner within Christos Creator Spirit that is all things, our multidimensional reality enviroments, and in all living animated life forms and their avatars, and in all encompassing nature of the Hyperdimensional Matrix of DNA Biotechnology.

The Breneau philosophy considerately acknowledges with Divine contemplation of the interdependence, interconnection and intrinsic value of all the encompassing components of animated physical and non physical reality, and the driving forces behind the components, and recognise that the living Christos Consciousness Spirit of Source is the tangible substance of Consciousness, of energy from which all things manifest and incarnate from, that are composed of the Energetic Divine Source Field, that is of the essence of Spirit.

The philosophy of the Christos Collectives knowledge refers to our personal individual Divine Temple Schematic Blueprint of the Living Creator Spirit Energy of which all beings, their avatars and all other things are manifested and created from. This wisdom is to give all races of species a chance to advance there personal growth Individually and as Consciousness Collectives, to gain empowerment genuinely through Spiritual development, regardless of there past affiliations with negative races or agendas or belief systems. These ancient teachings of wisdom are for all entities of the Divine energetic Spirit of Source, so that all beings can evolve back to their true Eternal nature of Spirit as Yanas Ascended Masters.

They teach an ancient advanced paradigm of perspective on the nature of reality, that goes beyond our Planet Gaia's Spiritual and scientific understandings, beyond the limitations of assumptions and conflicting philosophies we associate with them. These empowering ancient Cosmic Spiritual belief systems allow you to perceive the commonality and complementary Intrinsic association of all things, and that of the essence of Eternal Spirit. The knowledge at the heart of these teachings are derived from the Twelve ancient Holographical Cloister Dora Teura Plates that were created around 248,000BC, but also translated later on in the Five hundred and Sixty text books in the Indian Mahabharata Scriptures.

The Eieyani share this truth of the Founder races perspective of the Intrinsic nature of the Creation and the essence of Eternal Spirit with others in hope of seeing others advance in personal growth to achieve personal freedom, by passing this wisdom through reciprocal equal energy exchange, to those who show the intention of action with absolute pure sincerity. This ancient knowledge is available to all beings that are capable of translating information data from the Universal Unified field. The knowledge allows us to take a personal journey of inner knowing to discover an Intrinsic knowingness of significance of an everlasting shift in the empowerment of self Awareness, restoring our own inner avatar Christos Consciousness to our true nature of expression, then we can stand in our Eternal power to decide were and how we evolve, and to take responsibility for our Eieyani Elohim Oraphim Turaneusiam Angelic Human bloodline linerages DNA genepools.

So when I left my higher dimensional Planet and my extraterrestrial species and family to manifest on the Planet

Gaia, I teleported into my mothers womb to start this human manifestation in a three dimensional human avatar form, and I must say this can be a traumatic experience especially the birthing process. It also can be traumatic to wake up consciously with all the negative interference and genetic manipulation by negative spirits and entities with their own agenda's. Its also a traumatic experience to have to deal with waking up on a Planet in endless Wars, and traumatic to deal with the violation as an Eternal Interdimensional Source Light being to have be stifled by outside forces with their negative agenda's. I was born in the mid nineteen seventies when there was another wave of heavy negative draconian influence suppressing humanity, where a full militariation of the World occurred in secret and was in full motion, being directed by the negative intelligence agencies community from around the World, that were influenced, and mind controlled by the negative shapeshifters and races that live amongst us on the Planet, and off the Planet and from higher dimensions. When we recall our past as a child we can see the negative suppression by others like family, teachers, and via societies enforced rules and laws that go against nature itself, that held us down from being at our optimal creative expressions of ourselves in our true unstifled nature. Then there are also other outside forces of a negative spiritual form, and other extraterrestrial entities, and human military groups that also suppress and stifle our true nature, via many types of manipulation and interference and via phychic attacks. This is painful for us eternal angelic luminous beings being trapped in this human avatar as an infant and child, because these outside external influences of mixed messages and information is imprinting in our luminous energy fields, the software that informs our DNA the hardware. This means that ninty nine percent of this influence are violations to our rights of existence as eternal interdimensional luminous light beings. The other one percent is your loving connections and experiences of your family that nurtured and loved you, and talt you your values and the way to live life, these are the beautiful experiences from those around you as an infant and child, those that helped develop your consciousness on morality and on positive spiritual belief systems. They are the ones that had loving positive interactions with you from empathy and love that were very impactful in the right way. So this means that the ninty nine percent of influence that is almost everything else from the controlled external environment and influence from negative entities is a violation. Even the ridiculous way adults communicate with infants in a none sensical way like with sounds instead of clear adult

verbal communication or telepathic
communication, which is detrimental
programming, which is what many
adults do to guide their child, even
teaching the alphabet of languages,
which will spell bind the child into a
lower state of consciousness and belief
system, which helps further their
entrapment into the mind, into the
matrix of the mind, and then entraps
them further in their human avatar.
But we have to understand that this is
because the childs guardian has been
programmed and indoctrinated
through societies belief systems of
language of which there are many, and
we have to understand that language
has been used to control, segregate,
and spell bind humanity via vibrational
frequencies of the language itself. So
language has been weaponized by
negative races with their negative
agenda's for control and domination of
another species, because in our natural
states of consciousness we use telepathy
for communication via our psychic

abilities. So even these violations from the one's that loved and cared and nurtured us, slows and stops a child from evolving and interacting with spirit, other races, and the Universe's zero point energy field of the Holographical Hyperdimensional Light Time Templar Matrix of the Creation. These violations from loved ones and especially from the negative entities are violations that stop us interdimensional Source light beings in human physical form from fully interacting with the true nature of reality, the true nature of life its self, the true nature of existence. It denies our divine creative expression to manifest into the electromagnetic fields of the zero point energy fields of the Hyperdimensional Light Time Templar Matrix, and mainly allows us to manifest into the Planet Gaia's electromagnetic field. This is a massive violation that's happening to souls as an infant and child that ere manifesting on Planet Gaia, because it creates the discombobulation of the Infinite Consciousness of the child, this is the Infinite connection from their Collective previous manifested Star Systems. Like the positive Collectives of the Adromedan, Paladin, Alpha Centaurian, and the Acturian Star Systems of the Christos Source Collectives, which our their ancestors. And connections from the negative collectives like Zeta Reticuli and the Draconian Star Systems. This disconnects us from our other Star Systems languages that we carry with us as we incarnate on this Planet, its within our DNA, and disconnects us from our communication with them. So if we were not programmed and indoctrinated at conception we would naturally start to continue to communicate telepathically, and so be in a fifth density reality field of creative expression. But because we are genetically manipulated and live on a Planet within a society which pushes negative agenda polarities into humanities sub conscious mind, so that humans then create an illusionary state of fear, which comes from the manipulated emotional response to others and our environment, which manifests in the subconscious mind, bringing us into the fight, flight response. So humans then start to program psycho emotional fear based responses on our instinctive flight and fight responses, which are programmed into the infant and child on a continuum. Like when a child is constantly being told don't do that, you cant do that, restraining your growth and natural enlightened development, this is a violation to the eternal Interdimentional Source light being that has manifested in human form, it is a violation of their eternal sovereign spirit. Because every single time a boundary is set by an adult whether it be by a parent, gardian, teacher, or other citizen or authoritarian officer of the draconian society we live under, it is an absolute violation of the eternal spirit of the child. And like I mentioned earlier the adults are just doing what they were talt, what they were programmed and indoctrinated to believe was right, or what they just believe with no conscious awareness that it would have a negative effect on the growth of the conscious awareness of the child. Because the adults from family and our encompassing environment are just doing what they are predisposed to do, to guide, protect, and defend the child from harm. But this causes the effect of an energetic cage system prison around the fifth density connection of the infinite capacity of the child from the suppressive information collected and imprinted in their luminous energy field, which is the software that then informs the DNA, which is the hardware, which can then also manifest within the physical body in various forms of psychic mental illness or physical illness, if its from traumatic interactions and experiences. It can take half a life time to over come all the programming and indoctrination.

So when you go back to your experience of teleporting on to this World into your mothers womb and your conception, you have the realization of incarnation cycles as an eternal light being, and have to at some point of raising your conscious awareness look at your own genesis, the time when you manifested another experience into existence, your beginning of a new origin of creation into another manifested form. And from the perspective of manifesting in another species avatar form on another Planet in another dimension of the Holographical Hyperdimensional Light Time Templar Matrix, with also the realization that your true origins are from outside time and space in the eternal realms, that your from the Oneness ultra violet energetic plasma Source consciousness field, because Oneness is all there truly be in the eyes of Spirit.

But on the other hand you have to understand that because of the genetic manipulation of our twelve strands of DNA, with ten strands deactivated, turned off, and with access to only two strands of DNA, this has entrapped humanity into a duality reality of consciousness in the third dimension. So with humanity individually and collectivally at this time not being talt to control their minds, their emotions and thoughts, and with the orchestrated wars and violence on the Planet, it would be detrimental to other races out in the Universe and Interdimensionally, and for our human race if many traumatised souls on the Planet manifested their angry violent thoughts into the wider Creations zero point energy field, that would negatively affect other races in the Universe. So there is advanced draconian technology used to stop humanity manifesting into the wider Creations zero point electromagnetic energy field, and even if good forces of the Christos Collectives take control or have taken control of this advanced technology they cant just turn it off, because all of humaities thoughts would manifest into the Creation instantly in the negative and positive polarities. So it will proberly be removed when the ascensions fifth dimensional light flash process happens, were if your body is vibrating at the frequency of fifty one percent and above you will be shot out of your human avatar for thirty seconds while the fifth dimensional final stages of ascension occur, because you cannot be in your body on the Planet Gaia whilst the energetic light flash process occurs. Then we truly come into the age of Aquarius and come into a new way of being, a new way of creating and manifesting into the fabric of the Holographical Hyperdimensional Light Time Templar Matrix, then we can experience a new way of existence.

We now need and see new education facilities and sanctuaries being manifested over the Planet to teach the next generations and guide them in the right spiritual teachings and direction of ancient knowledge and wisdom, like schools of sacred geometry, Chinese medicine, Ayurvedic teachings and medicines, Buddhist teachings, and Shamanic teachings of Universal Chi energy, and Shamanic ceremonies, and plant medicines, and the importance of strict diets. Along with other teachings of Reki energy medicine, acupuncture, meditation, yoga, chakra alignment healing, sound healing, and of martial arts like QiGong, Tai Chi, and other energy arts and practices. Also with other teachings of calm peaceful manifestations through mind disciplines, and teachings of quantum physics education, astrology, fractal geometry, and astrophysics. Also teachings on the subconscious mind and conscious mind, and on the chakra energy systems, the pineal gland, pineal chakra and about activating their light filament pineal antenna's, and teachings of their Merkaba light Body. This will allow the students natural fulfilment of genious to fullfill itself, in a natural self revealing, self fulfilling, and self manifesting complex way. This allows the spirit to evolve in the direction that it naturally gravitates to, and this does not stifle the students growth spiritually, mentally, emotionally, or physically, but instead allows the student to blossom. It is the complete opposite of todays draconian education system in society at present, that is built from draconian education systems that the Anunnaki Illuminati and Masonic orders have put in place in the Planet's corrupt education systems, that promote and teach false inversions of the truth of the eight fundamental principles of Creation. They teach false inversions of reality because they have hijacked and manipulated the education system, because you do not define an education system with a curriculum that is a false illusion of reality, because this stifles a

being, stifles a students optimal
potential into their divine higher states
of consciousness. And stifles their
direct access and communication to
their extraterrestrial connections to
their different Star System families,
and disconnects them from the zero
point energy field of the Holographical
Hyperdimensional Light Time
Templar Matrix. This is a direct
intentional violation of the rights of a
manifesting luminous light being on
this Planet Gaia, that wants to be in
their true nature and express and
explore and expand into this World
with their full creative potential. But
instead we are stifled by inhabitions
and prohabitions, which then can take
half a life time to deprogram from your
subconscious mind and delete this false
illusion of reality from your luminous
energy field, and delete the negative
non serving cycles that you were
operating under in a low vibrational
resonance within the negative polarity.
And then you can reinform your

luminous energy field with positive cycles into higher vibrations of resonance, which in turn reinforms your DNA, and then you can consciously evolve to grow a new body, from the divine schematic blueprint of information within your DNA. That means you will then live, heal, and die differently, until you access your fully activated Mer-Ka-Ba field, your Eternal Human Light Body.

CHAPTER TWO

The Pineal Gland

The Pineal Gland is a small endocrine gland found in most vertebrates, which produces melatonin in humans, located in the epithalamus, in a groove where the two halves of the thalamus join, its shape and size resembles a pine nut, after which it is named. The pineal gland produces melatonin, a serotonin derived hormone which modulates sleep patterns in both circadian and seasonal cycles, and the pineal gland, endocrine gland is the source of melatonin a hormone derived from tryptophan that plays a central role in the regulation of circadian rhythum, which is the roughly twenty four hour cycle of biological activities associated with natural periods of light and darkness. So the anatomy of the pineal gland which develops from the roof of the diencephalon, a section of the brain, and is located behind the third cerabral ventricle in the brain midline between the two cerebral hemispheres. Its name is derived from its shape, which is similar to that of a pine cone, in Latin pinea, and in adult humans its size is about 0.8 cm or 0.3 inch long and weighs approximately 0.1 gram or 0.004 ounce. The pineal gland has a rich supply of adrenergic nerves, neurons sensitive to the adrenal hormone, that greatly influence its function. Microscopically the gland is composed of pinealocytes, rather typical endocrine cells except for extensions that mingle with those of adjacent cells, and supporting cells that are similar to the astrocytes of the brain. In humans small deposits of calcium often make the pineal body visible on X-rays, this is because of bad calcium consumption, which leads to the pineal gland eventually becoming more or less calcified in most people, with an oyster like shell of calcium enveloping the pineal gland. Which stops humans using their third eye vision and disconnects them from the zero point energy field of Creation, which also stops us communicating psychically with our Star families in other Solar Systems. But in some lower vertebrates the gland has a well developed eye like structure, but in others though not organized and working at its full potential it is an eye that only functions as a light receptor. The pineal hormones of both melatonin and its precursor, serotonin, which are derived chemically from the alkaloid substance tryptamine, are synthesized in the pineal gland. Along with other brain sites the pineal gland also produces neurosteroids, Dimethyltryptamine known as DMT, a hallucinogenic compound present in the Amazonian botanical drink Ayahuasca which is made from several species of Banisteriopsis Caapi, a South American jungle vine, that is chemically similar to melatonin and serotonin, and is considered to be a trace substance in human blood and urine. It is also produced by the pineal gland and the DMT has been detected in human pineal microdialysates, purified pineal extracts, and its been proven that it regulates biosynthesis in the mammalian pineal gland. The pineal gland in ancient texts is also known as the Gateway of the Soul, and the Seat of the Soul.

In addition to the pineal gland, melatonin is also synthesized in the vertebrate retina, where it transduces information about environmental light through local receptors designated MT1 and MT2, and in certain other tissues, such as the gastrointestinal tract and the organ of the skin. In the general rate limiting step of melatonin biosynthesis, an enzyme called serotonin N-acetyltransferase, AANAT catalyzes the conversion of serotonin to

N-acetylserotonin. Subsequently that compound is catalyzed to melatonin by acetylserotonin *O*-methyltransferase, ASMT. The rise in circulating melatonin concentrations that occurs and is maintained after sun down and with darkness coincides with the activation of AANAT during dark periods. Melatonin concentrations also are higher in the cerebrospinal fluid of the third ventricle of the brain than in the cerebrospinal fluid of the fourth ventricle or in the blood. That suggests that melatonin is also secreted directly into the cerebrospinal fluid, where it can have direct and sustained effects on target areas of the central nervous system. In some species pineal cells are photo sensitive, and in humans and higher mammals there is a photo endocrine system made up of the retina, the suprachiasmatic nucleus of the hypothalamus, and noradrenergic sympathetic fibres, the neurons responsive to the neurotransmitter norepinephrine, terminating in the pineal that provides light and circadian information that regulates pineal melatonin secretion. In contrast to many other endocrine hormones, human melatonin concentrations are highly variable, and serum melatonin levels decline markedly during childhood, as there is little or no growth of the pineal gland after about one year of age. The pineal physiology and pathophysiology which consists of circulating melatonin levels in vertebrates are derived from pineal melatonin secretion, and their magnitude informs brain regions about environmental light-dark cycles and seasonality, as inferred by changes in the duration of the nocturnal melatonin plateau. Those cues in turn help to entrain sleep activity which is enhanced by darkness, and reproductive cycle events are also increased with more seasonal lighting.

However now we come to discussing how to activate the pineal gland, we're now shifting into the psychological and spiritual arena. It is clear to see how the above listed attributes are also essential for our spiritual and psychological development, for instance how can one hope to get to know their own personal inner self shadow without clarity, intuition, and focus, because the pineal gland activation brings us a more significant connection to the natural World, it can also lead to a willingness to let go of many ego pursuits that are incongruent with our Soul. Lucid dreaming, astral projection, and a more vivid imagination are also topics related to pineal gland activation, and in fact, the pineal is a gateway to higher creativity and experience. In ancient times different cultures knew about the pineal gland like in ancient Egypt with the Eye of Ra that depicted a cross section of the pineal gland on the left in the next image, and on the right side of the next image the pituitary, and corpus cailosum region are also shown.

And even though modern science and medicine have just begun to understand the critical role of the pineal gland, all the ancient cultures and traditions already have this knowledge. For Buddhists, the pineal is a symbol of spiritual awakening, and in Hinduism, the pineal is the seat of intuition and clairvoyance, and for Taoists, the pineal is the mind's eye or heavenly eye, and in ancient Egypt, we find numerous references to the third eye and the pineal region, and third eye symbolism is found throughout Egyptian, Buddhist, Vedic, Hindu, and all tribal societies and cultures mythology. The pineal gland is also known as the Seat of the Soul and in the bible it was stated in Matthew 6.22 that, the light of the body is the eye, if therefore thine eye be single, thy whole body shall be full of light, and in this text its telling you by its wording of how eye is singular and thine eye be single, that its referring to the pineal gland all seeing eye. And the ancient Greeks believed the pineal was our connection to thought itself, Herophilus described it as the sphincter of thought. Also the french mathematician and philosopher Rene Descartes shared this view about the pineal gland, he wrote in Treatise of Man, My view is that this gland is the principle Seat of the Soul, and the place which all thoughts are formed. For thousands of years in both the western and eastern parts of the World, the pineal gland has been

viewed as a connecting link between
the physical three dimensional World
and the psychic fifth dimensional
plane, and beyond with a link
connecting to the eternal realms
outside time and space. Below is the
sketch known as Seat of the rational
Soul, which was composed and drawn
by Rene Descates of the pineal gland
and the third eye.

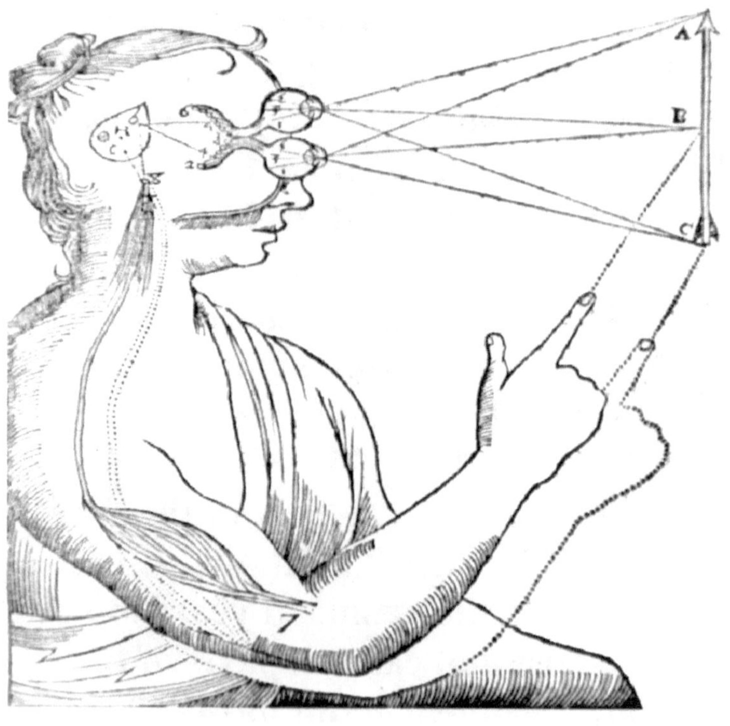

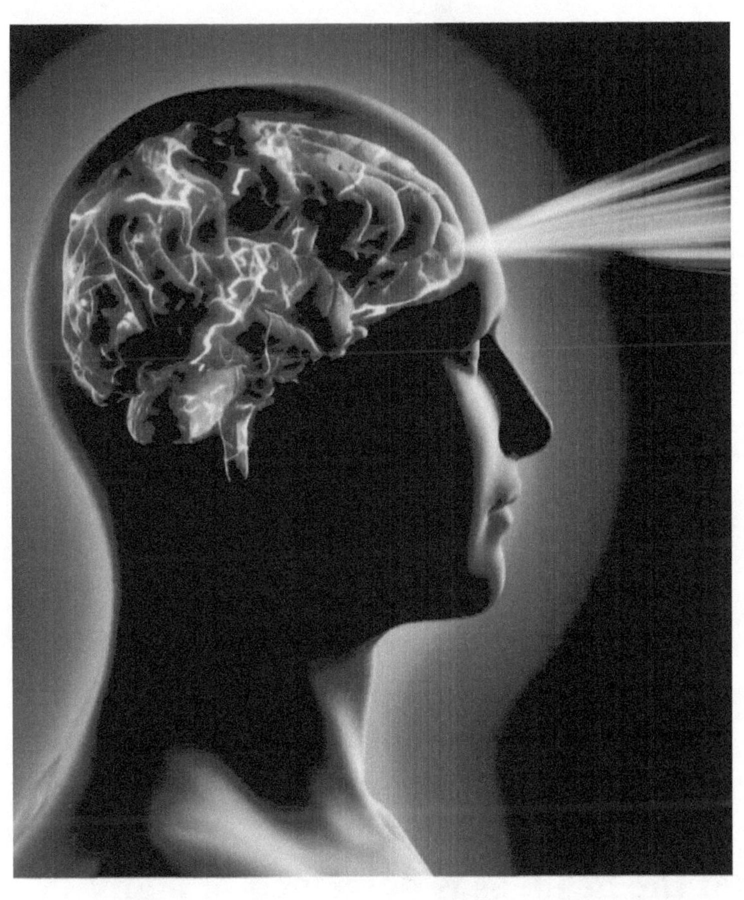

The pineal gland was called the third eye by ancient tribal indigenous cultures that referred to the pineal as the inner eye or the third eye. When you cut the pineal open, pinealocytes line the interior, these pinealocytes resemble the rods and cones in the retina of our eyes, the pineal even has retinal tissue and the same physical wiring as the brain's visual cortex. This explains that light stimulates the pineal in creatures like birds, lizards, and fish directly through the skull, in many reptiles the pineal has all the photoreceptive elements characteristic of an eye. So its therefore referred to as a third eye because in many species it resembles an eye in both structure and activity, but however in mammals, light stimulates the pineal exclusively via the eyes. Our ancient ancestors believed humans initially received light stimulation through the top of the head at the crown of the head through the crown chakra six inches above the top of the head, as is described in many ancient traditions. The pineal gland represents the inward seeing eye, so this means that activating this third eye allows us to see life beyond the typical limitations of our perception, bringing clarity of vision, then being able to perceive beyond the illusion of light and perceive the multidimensional fields of realities in the Universe, and beyond in the holographical hyperdimensional light time templar matrix of Creation, and beyond outside space and time in the eternal realms, and to also percieve the ultra violet Source Collective Oneness field.

So how do we start to activate the pineal gland, well each tradition has different methods for activating the third eye, and it may resonate differently with other methods for different individuals based on type, temperament, or some other mental or physical factors. Here are five Pineal gland activation methods below, they are Meditation, Qigong, Psychedelics, Brainwave Frequencies, and Sun Gazing. The third eye is designed to open naturally when the aligned conditions are appropriate for an individual. In ancient cultures they had Shamans who guided such processes for the younger generations, and taught them all their wisdom and knowledge of spirit, nature, plant medicines, energy practices, and transcendental meditation and travel. But today we are responsible for our own inner journeys to awaken and evolve the inner development of our consciousness, so we can access our core energy systems and light body.

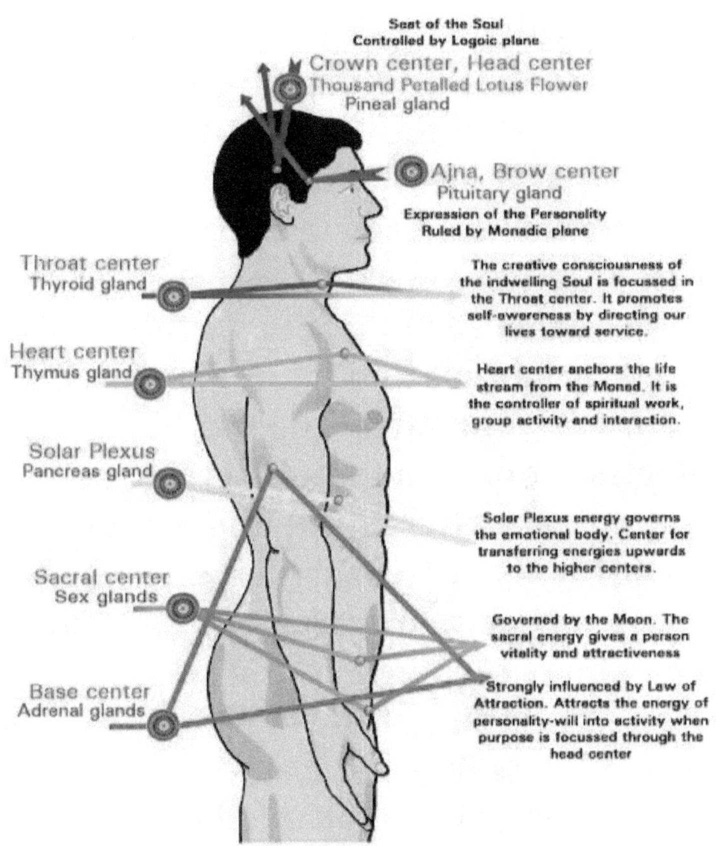

Method one for pineal gland activation is meditation, because the most traditional method of opening your third eye is through normal Lotus position sitting meditation, and it is an essential daily practice to access your highest potential. But there are various meditative techniques that you can use and practice to stimulate and activate

your pineal gland directly. So the
pineal gland is also sensitive to the
bioelectrical signals of light and dark
in its environment, and meditation can
activate this bioelectric energy and
with practice you can direct this energy
via your focused attention to the pineal
gland by stimulating it and helping it to
open. For your meditation to be
effective your mind must become still,
so that the scattered fluctuating energy
in your body can consolidate, so we
have to observe or watch our mind and
then allow it to become still without
effort, by letting go of the thoughts,
then stillness will come, and later
clarity prevails. So for third eye
meditation you sit in a comfortable
lotus sitting position, if you are not able
to flex and bend your legs sit on a chair
with spine straight in an upright
posture, and with your fingers linked
or hands linked and feet crossed, this is
to allow the energy to flow in the body.
Then close your eyes, and focus on
your breath with deep and slow intakes

of air, so your breathing slows down, you will become calmer and even more relaxed, then focus your attention onto your third eye just above the eye line in the center of the forehead in a deeply relaxed state. There are also other techniques that you can use like to visulize that your crown chakra is connected to Source and see white light coming into your crown chakra six inches above your head, and see white light coming up from Mother Earths center chakra coming up into your base chakra up the spine into the head, so you are connected, and then visualize that you're breathing a golden white light through the center of your third eye. The main thing is to remain relaxed and avoid trying to force the practiced exercise, and also let go of expecting any result, because this can create tension that will block the flow of energy in this process. **This meditation works** by placing your focused attention on the pineal gland, you are focusing your internal core chi energy on this regions location, the Chinese call it Yi, or attention.

This relaxed focus attention releases neuropeptides and nitric oxide, which trigger the relaxation response, and these chemicals will allow you to move into a deeper meditation state while stimulating the third eye location. Now melatonin is an essential hormone produced and circulated by the pineal gland, and we know that in the brains of practicing meditators, they find an increase in melatonin secretion. You will know if your third eye meditation is working when you begin to feel either a slight pressure in this pineal region location and or a pulsating sensation, which will feel as though there is a mini heart beating in your forehead at the third eye location, it will be a new sensation initially the first few times it starts activating.

Method two for pineal gland activation is Qigong, and Qigong translates to life energy skill or energy cultivation. These Qigong exercises are designed to increase the dedicated practitioner's sensitivity to the flow of energy within the body, called Chi or Qi, one learns how to move this internal Chi energy with gentle physical motions and breathing, resulting in the practitioner learning how to move this inner Chi energy with one's mind with your focused intention of Yi. Many people have many blocked energy meridians and energy centers that keep the body's inner core Chi from reaching vital glands in the endocrine system. So focused attention on circulating the body's energy using Qigong really helps to access and open these pathways to allow this internal core Chi energy to reach these areas and activate the pineal gland. This type of meditation practice that's described is actually a form of Qigong, because you are focusing your iniention on the pineal gland to increase the inner concentrated Chi energy flow into this regions location. When you have developed the sensitivity to your body's energy through some Qigong energy practice, it will be more effective when you start to practice this meditation. So if you practice energy practices like Qigong or Tai Chi on a daily basis then your body's energy systems and there energy flows will open up naturally, and then you will experience an increased flow of Chi core energy flowing throughout your body's merdian and chakra energy systems, and through the brain synapses, which are the small gaps at the end of a neuron, that allows a signal to pass from one neuron to the next, they will be able to process more energy light information faster. These neurons are the cells that transmit light information between your brain and other parts of your central nervous system, these synapses are found where neurons connect with other neurons. These types of activated pineal gland meditation experieces can be like a vivid vision that you can have when you part take in a Shamanic

Ayahuasca ceremony and ingest the sacred medicinal plant medicine.

Method three for pineal gland activation, is Phychedelics like DMT. So the pineal gland synthesizes and secretes a hormone called melatonin, but the pineal is also responsible for another really important chemical known as N,N-dimethyltryptamine or better known as DMT, and DMT is also known as the Spirit Molecule, which is a natural hallucinogen capable of producing extraordinary visions and mystical states of higher consciousness. DMT is similar to the properties of lysergic acid diethylamide, which is known as Acid or LSD, but it is naturally occurring in our body, where as LSD is a synthetic produced drug. Also DMT exists in all of our bodies and occurs throughout the plant spirit and animal spirit kingdoms, and it is part of the normal makeup of human beings and other mammals, like marine animals, and the grasses, and amphibians, and the fungi, barks, roots and flowers. It is also known that the brain transports DMT across the blood brain barrier into its tissues. DMT is not an insignificant or irrelevant by product of our metabolism, because the brain goes out of its way to draw it into its confines, to feed of that light information energy, because DMT is the lens of the pineal gland that allows us to see wider encompassing layers of other dimensions of our surrounding reality that are usually not accessible to us. DMT is present in the Amazonian botanical medicine brew called Ayahuasca, which is a sacred medicinial brew made from the vine of the Ayahuasca plant combined with the leaves of either Chagropanga or Chacruna bush. It is known that a minimal amount of DMT is produced by the pineal gland every night while we dream, and when you take Ayahuasca you are getting a massive DMT boost that helps to break up any calcification existing around your pineal gland. This plant medicine is ingested as part of a South American Shamanic ceremony that leads participants through profound experiences of both positive and negative, but you heal and learn from the negative as well and can let go of trauma through some of the negative expriences, because this content of old non serving cycles in your subconscious mind can be broken and you then you come into conscious awareness to move forward. And when it is used in the proper intentional mindset and ceremonial environment setting, Ayahuasca and other substances like Peyote, Iboga, and Psilocybin magic mushrooms have the potential to heal and expand our minds and activate our pineal glands. And injesting preparation diet medicinal plants before taking these psychedelic substances is normal protocal, and then going into isolation which is known as tambo, this allows silence, which creates stillness allowing clarity to come into your awareness, and awareness of your pineal gland and your overall state of enheightened consciousness.

Method four for pineal gland activation is via brainwave frequencies, because our brains operate on a range of brainwave patterns, and each pattern establishes a particular state of consciousness, with low frequencies keeping you in a lower negative subconsciousness awareness state, and higher frequency brainwaves allow higher states of conscious awareness. So from high to low here are the most commonly cited brainwave frequencies and their associated states of consciousness in the next images, of Gamma brainwaves at 30-100Hz, Beta brainwaves at 14-30Hz, then Alpha brainwaves at 9-13Hz, then Theta brainwaves at 4-8Hz, and Delta brainwaves at 1-3Hz.

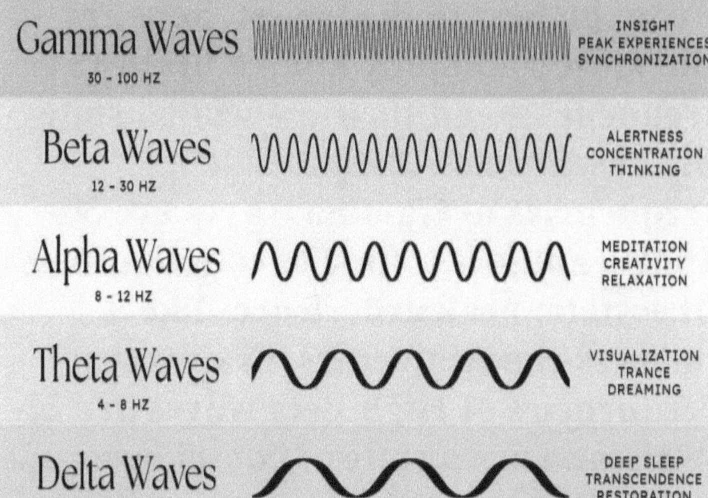

Gamma Waves
30 - 100 HZ
INSIGHT
PEAK EXPERIENCES
SYNCHRONIZATION
Beta Waves
12 - 30 HZ
ALERTNESS
CONCENTRATION
THINKING
Alpha Waves
8 - 12 HZ
MEDITATION
CREATIVITY
RELAXATION
Theta Waves
4 - 8 HZ
VISUALIZATION
TRANCE
DREAMING
Delta Waves
0.5 - 4 HZ
DEEP SLEEP
TRANSCENDENCE
RESTORATION

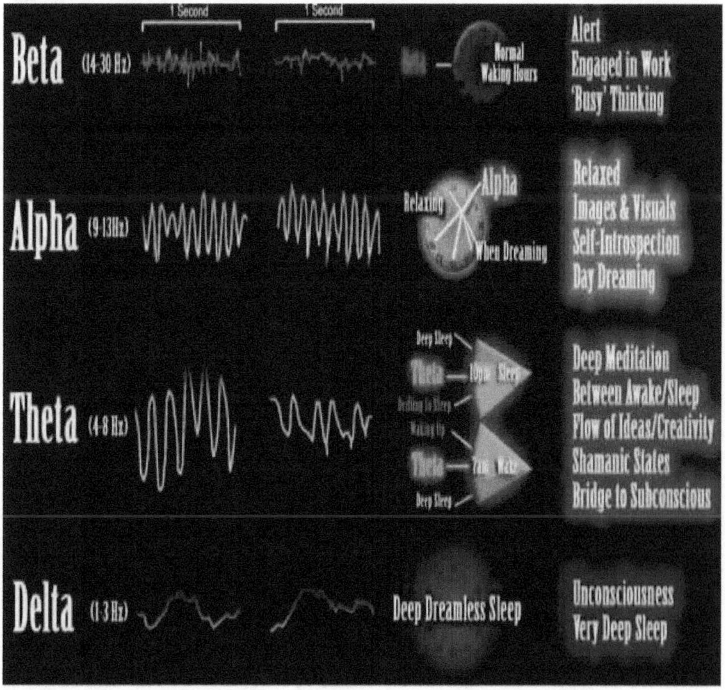

1 Second
1 Second
Beta (14-30 Hz)
Normal Waking Hours
Alert
Engaged in Work
'Busy' Thinking
Alpha (9-13Hz)
Relaxing
Alpha
When Dreaming
Relaxed
Images & Visuals
Self-Introspection
Day Dreaming
Theta (4-8 Hz)
Deep Sleep
Theta
Light Sleep
Drifting to Sleep
Waking Up
Theta
Deep Sleep
Deep Meditation
Between Awake/Sleep
Flow of Ideas/Creativity
Shamanic States
Bridge to Subconscious
Delta (1-3Hz)
Deep Dreamless Sleep
Unconsciousness
Very Deep Sleep

From highest to the lowest, here are the most commonly known brainwave frequencies and their associated state of consciousness. Brainwave frequencies of Gamma waves are 30-100Hz and are a state of consciousness of ecstatic peak experiences like oneness connectiveness, brainwave frequencies of High Beta waves are 22-40Hz and are a state of consciousness of anxiety and nervousness, brainwave frequencies of Low Beta are 14-22Hz and are a state of consciousness of alertness and focus, brainwave frequencies of Alpha are 8-14Hz and are a state of consciousness of being physically relaxed and in meditive states, brainwave frequencies of Theta Waves are 4-8Hz and are a state of consciousness of being deeply relaxed and of rapid eye movement in sleep state, and brainwave frequencies of Delta are 0.5-4Hz and are a state of consciousness of dreamless sleep and of the deepest meditive meditation states.

For third eye activation you can get many types of brainwave audio programs, these programs are usually a combination of binaural beats and isochronic tones, because when you simultaneously hear one pure tone sine wave in the left ear and another sine wave in the right ear, it creates an auditory illusion known as a binaural tone or beat, and an isochronic tone is merely a pure tone that is turned on and off rapidly. The objective of these programs is to induce a particular state of consciousness by training the brain to the frequencies of the sounds, this does facilitate a change in brainwave patterns and has a therapeutic healing effect, and the best benefits from brainwave frequencies come when used in conjunction with meditation practices.

So which brainwave frequencies are used for the pineal gland activation, well two individuals during an Ayahuasca DMT ceremonial experience found that they produced an increase in global electroencephalogram coherence in the 36-44 Hz and 50-64 Hz frequency band width ranges, and these frequency band widths are known as Gamma waves. So what brainwave frequencies are consistent with the production of the pineal glands main chemical melatonin, so the answer is Delta waves, the brain waves we experience during deep dreamless sleep. Also active during the rapid eye movement stage of sleep are Theta waves, so both Gamma and Theta waves work together during the rapid eye movement sleep state. So we need to use brainwave frequencies for Pineal gland activation, by using binaural beats and isochronic tones that specifically activate Delta, Theta, and Gamma frequencies.

Method five for pineal gland activation, is Sun Gazing. This next method, if you are unfamiliar with it, might seem odd and perhaps dangerous, because we have all been told not that staring directly straight at the sun or it will damage our eyes, but sun gazing is a powerful, well known ancient technique with tremendous benefits, and the basic theory behind sun gazing is that you are absorbing the energy from the sun directly through your eyes and skin. Through sun gazing many have been able to go long periods even years without eating and remain physically healthy. These claims that people have survived mostly on sunlight with a minimal amount of water have been verified. Neuroscientists and pineal gland specialists have studied sun gazing during a one hundred and thirty day period, and they found that the grey cells in the brain are actually regenerating and found that the pineal gland was expanding in size. Its also been reported in research that sunlight reduces the harmful effects of artificial blue light, and that the sun's direct light intake helps restore the original size and function of the pineal gland.

Then there is also the huge benefits of Fasting and while stopping eating is not the goal of pineal gland activation, many who have practiced sun gazing have reported that it reduces hunger, and fasting reduces the risk of diabetes and heart disease, it also increases human hormone growth, and lowers cholesterol levels in the bloodstream. The human growth hormone is a metabolic protein that protects lean muscle and metabolic balance, and these hormones increased in an average of one thousand and four hundred percent in women and two thousand percent in men during a twenty four hour period of fasting, and moderate fasting also supports detoxification which can be the most significant benefit to your pineal gland and over all health.

Society has told that it is very dangerous to look at the sun directly because of ultraviolet UV radiation that can damage the eyes retina, but did you know that the UV index is usually zero during the sunrise and sunset period. So when sun gazing it is important to only look at the sun within the first hour of sunrise in the morning and the last hour in the evening when the sun still has an orange glow, that is why you do not sun gaze during the day when the UV index is very high. The best method is for you to start sun gazing within the first fifteen minutes of sunlight in the morning and the last fifteen minutes at the end of the day during the sunset, to start you only gaze into the sun for a couple of seconds at first, then build up to forty five minutes per day after nine months of practice. But even even occasional sungazing in the early morning or late evening will support your efforts to activate your pineal gland.

So ultimately all of the pineal gland activation methods discussed are to bring the entire brain online in full coherence to activate the pineal gland, it chakra and its antenna light rods, to activate the human heads light sphere that encompasses the head, and connects to your Merkaba human light field.

This is an **MRI** image below of the brain on **LSD DMT.**

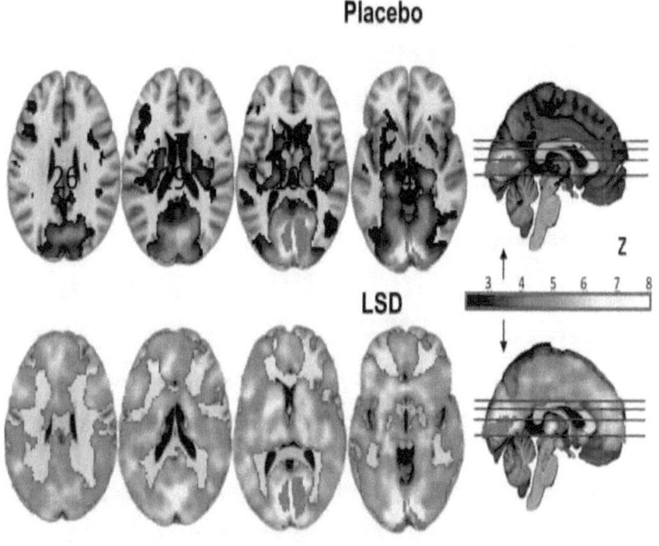

The brain scan image represents the goal of these methods to activate the whole brain, including the pineal gland.

But one must remember that the pineal gland activation is meant to be something that happens naturally, and when we discuss pineal gland activation, we are talking about bringing the entire brain online and integrating all the various brain regions into one cohesive working unit, to give us the ability to raise the frequency of the brain and change the physical structure of our entire consciousness over time. And as the pineal gland activates and the brain becomes more integrated, you begin to perceive your encompassing reality very differently, because you will begin to notice more of your negative unconscious cycles of behaviorial patterns, which helps you get to know your inner shadow, the negative part of your own ego, and everything becomes more vivid, including the realities of your inner internal World. You will wake up consciously to many other new realities around you in life with many other encompassing realities of the Universe and existence itself, that were not available to you before accessing your pineal gland and higher states of consciousness, as new way of being comes into your life experiences.

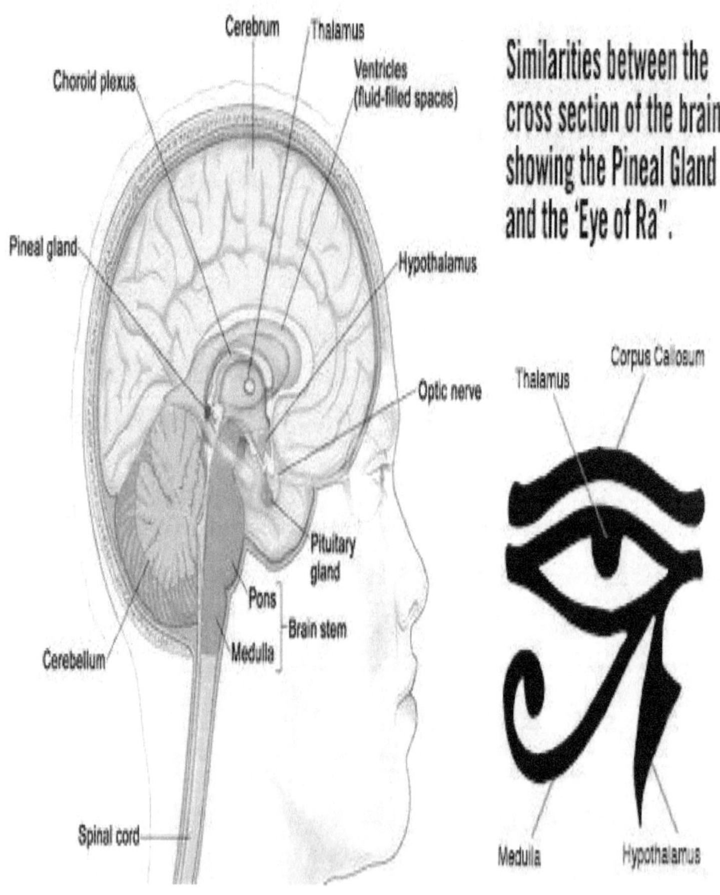

The Pineal Gland Is Activated Through The Chakra System Into A Unifed Field

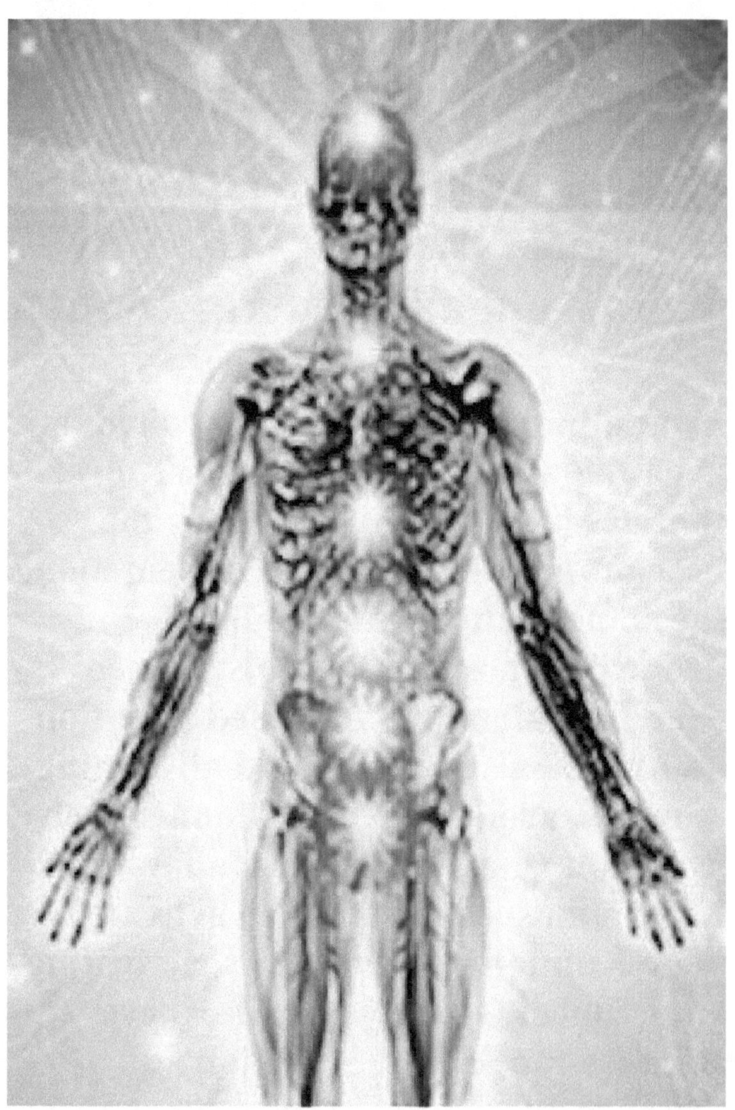

CHAPTER THREE

An Introduction To Your Pineal Gland Activated By Your Kundalini Energy System

Kundalini means circular or coiled, in yoga the word applies to the life force that lies like a coiled serpent at the base of the spine, that can be sent along the spine to the head through prescribed postures and disciplined exercises, along with focused attention on breath, a strict diet, and abstaining from sex around the full Moon's twelve cycles on your Star sign, to allow your Kundalini seed fluid oils to activate your Kundalini energy flow, activating your Pineal Gland, your Third eye. Because the Sacred Secretion and Cerebrospinal fluid activate the Christ within, accessing your Christos Eternal Human Angelic Light Body, via the schematic blueprint within your DNA. It's the Sacred oil Secretion that activates your ten dormant strands of DNA, activating your Mer Ka Ba field, your Human Light Body field.

The anointing is the Secretion, a substance once named Chrism, the origin of the word Christ being, anointing or anointed. The Christ within us all is born in the Sacred Plexus, known as the, Sacred Place, where the five fused vertebrae of the spine meet, this is where the Christ seed is born and begins its journey up the thirty three vertebrae to be Crucified, meaning amplified in power, and it's amplified in power by a thousand fold. When it meets the Pituitary and Pineal Gland, it sits there for two and a half days in the Hypothalamus, known as the tomb, it creates a circuit causing the Secretion of DMT, referred to as the Honey, and Serotonin, referred to as the Milk.

When the seed and oil is preserved and returned creating a higher vibrational circuit, you can reach the Promised land and Ascend, because you have activated your Kundalini energy flow systems, and you become an intune antenna connecting to the Zero Point Energy field, accessing higher dimensions of Consciousness, transcending the Templar light time Hyperdimensional Matrix of the three Primal Sound fields of the Creation, (created by the Yanas Ascended Masters) that's projected from the Oneness of the Eternal energetic Ultra Violet Source field Consciousness Collective. So activating your Kundalini oil Secretion and activating your Kundalini energy systems allows you to access the Christ Body within, accessing your Eternal Diamond Sun Angelic Human Light Body, allowing you to walk through the gates of Nirvana.

Raising the Chrism, Santa Claus, Joseph Mary and the Crucifiction, the

Pineal Gland known as Joseph, secrets the Milk, and the Pituitary known as Mary secrets the Honey, both are from the same source, the Claustrum, known as Santa Claus. The two Sacred oils travel down into the Solar Plexus via the semi-lunar Ganglion Pneumogastric nerve. The psycho-physical germ, the fruit of the Tree of Life, is born in the Solar Plexus, known as the Manger. The Ida (red), and the Pingala (blue), the two nerve fluids, where at the cossing of the Medulla Oblongata, the Crucifiction takes place where it rests for around two and a half days. The Sacred oil returns after crossing the Crucifiction and it enters the Cerebellum, Golgotha, the place of the skull, where the Kundalini oil fluid, known as the Christ fluid is refined and multiplied by a thousand fold. Allowing you to access your Physiological Regeneration capabilities, via your DNA repairing RNA systems, allowing you to rapidly heal your Angelic Human physical

Avatar, instantly repairing and healing your biological body.

It is also stated in ancient scripture that if, you love righteousness, and hate wickedness, then therefore God, your God, you your internal light being Spirit of God, will anoint you with the oil of gladness above your fellows, your fellow man. When people have felt the Kundalini process activating within themselves, they say they feel the anointing coming over them, and when people say that what they actually mean is the presence of God, but sometimes that presence is felt as if they have been anointed in a physical sense due to righteous living, because they have preserved a physical substance that in turn anoints their minds, and gifts their third sight. So if we live a righteous life, a positive mindset lifestyle, and if we practice a level of discipline of our minds and body's, we will be anointed internally, and the Secretion that comes from the Claustrum, which travels down the thirty three vertebraes and returns up to the skull, crossing the Vegus nerve, meeting with the Pituitary and Pineal Gland, and at that point it sits in the Hypothalamus, known as the tomb, just as Jesus did for two and a half days, then the Honey and Milk Kundalini oils rise and it is Crucified and amplified in power, it then Ascends to the Promise land flowing to the Pineal Gland, that secrets Serotonine and DMT, this puts you in a high vibratory state.

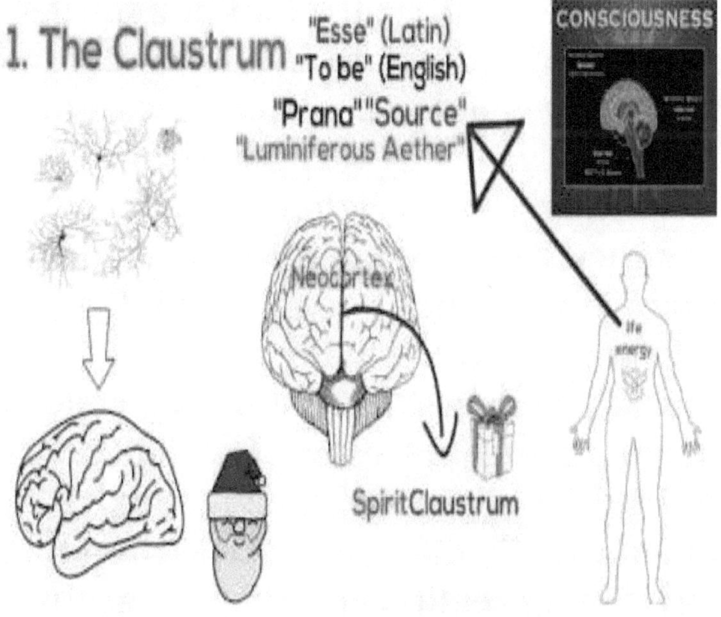

Then your mental state of clarity is profound, your in a blissful thoughtless state, in a state of being perfectly present, this is what the anointing process is, and would benefit our Planetary body as a whole if all of humanity could live with morality, by living in a moral manner in our daily lifes in the present continuum moments of now, living by the moral guidance code of the Sacred spoken word of vibration, that creates living animated Geomancy, living three dimensional Sacred geomentry, the building blocks of the Scaffolding of Life. So if humanity could live presently with the quality of morality being in accord with standards of right or good conduct, by a system of a collection of ideas of right and wrong conduct, a Virtuous conduct, living by a set of moral principles derived from a code of conduct from Cosmic, Sacred, Spiritual philosophy, then humanity could rapidly change their surrounding enveloping reality, creating a peaceful magical World of wonder for all to Co-Create in and share. These principles are from the Vedas teachings, they are Sacred ancient Indian texts, the Vedas are the religious texts which inform the religion of Hinduism, also known as Sanatan Dharma, meaning Eternal Order or Eternal Path, the term Veda means Knowledge, because they contain the fundamental knowledge relating to the underlying cause of, function of, and personal response to existence. It is also known that the religion of Buddhism and its teachings were birthed out of the ancient texts and teachings of the Vedic Sanskrit texts from the Hinduism religion, that are the ancient texts of knowledge and wisdom, to guide you on your eternal path back to your eternal embodied state of being, in this Divine Angelic Human Avatar, your Divine Temple of Man. The process of man going from being a physical and human creature, to becoming an Immortal and glorified child of the Most High, known in theological terms as Theosis, this ancient Christian concept refers to the Spiritual process that occurs resulting in the Deification of Man. It is also known in Shamanic practices, in their ancient knowledge and wisdom teachings as the process of evolving from Homo-Sapian to Homo-Luminous, where a human being accesses his or her Mer Ka Ba field, accessing their Human Light Body.

The Rebirth= As your cerebral spinal fluid (Christ) climbs your 33 Vertebrae(Jacobs Ladder) and meets your 12 cranial nerves(12 disciples) it ignites the pineal gland which is your resurrection.

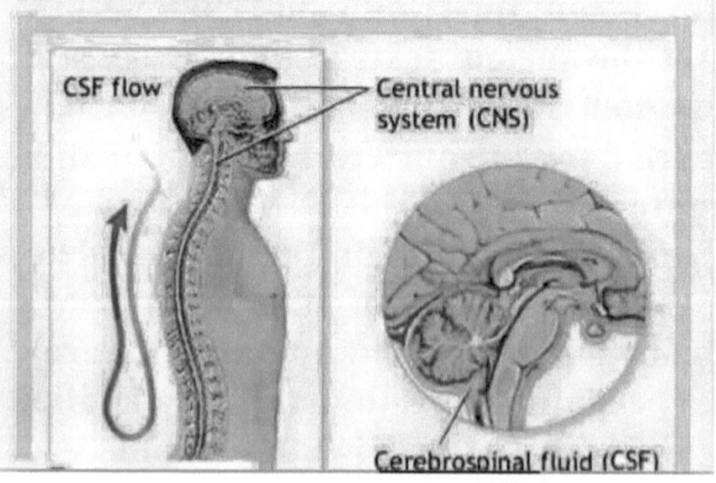

So if humans individually can live by the moral guidance code like the normative ethical philosophy of the Golden Rule, which states, one should treat others as one would like others to treat oneself, and whilst embracing at the same time and preserving that internal anointing of the Kundalini oil fluids, embracing the Kundalini energy, this will then change a human being forever, because they will no longer be in the low vibration of temptation and sin, they will then be vibrating at a higher frequency in a higher state of Consciousness allowing them to evolve to Homo-Luminous. So if we live with disciplined daily Spiritual practices, with diet and fasting, and with good will and intentions to ourselves and others, and with pure positive thoughts, we can activate the Christ Kundalini energy within to activate the Chrism, to become anointed from within activating your Third Eye Chakra, and then when this process occurs you access and open a door to a new way of being, of existing, of experiencing, then accessing our Diamond Sun Light Body.

This occurs because we tune into and access a different higher vibrational frequency, this allows us to move beyond this low physical density reality, this lower vibrational Consciousness state. So by tuning into nature and by connecting to Spirit, with Sacred disciplines and practices, and with meditation and diet, this raises your internal Chi energy system igniting your Kundalini oil fluids, allowing you to anoint yourself personally, with focused will and attention, we all have this Eternal Light Body activation potential. So we must practice anointing ourselves every full Moon cycle, then we become more energized and focused with our attention clear, that's directed by clarity, as our Consciousness rises, as we become more focused with our attention in the present moment. Our channels are then open to the Ether energy fields of Spirit, and we are then able to access the Zero Point Energy field, this allows us to be able to manipulate matter and manifest via our intention of focused Kundalini Chi energy, at a different faster rate of manifestation. So to save ourselves from this lower three dimensional reality which is a lower state of Consciousness, we must activate the Christ seed within, the true meaning of the word to be saved by Christ is internal, this can be manifested individually because the foundations are in place for it to happen today on the Planet, because this ancient knowledge and wisdom of the process of the Sacred Secretion of the Kundalini oil fluids rising and activating the Kundalini energy system, activating the Pituitary and Pineal gland, activating your Third eye, and in turn your Mer Ka Ba human light body. This knowledge is hidden within all of the religions of the

World, it is there to be deciphered, which it has been and is being shared by many Souls all over the Planet, these Souls have manifested onto the Planet from the many species and races of the Christos Consciousness Collectives, that are members of the Interdimensional Association of Free Worlds, manifesting on the Planet to make a difference for humanity from within, by teaching and sharing ancient wisdom, to raise Consciousness, and by activating their own Sacred Secretion, activating their Kundalini energy, to access and open their Eternal Angelic Human Light Body, to raise the human Collectives Consciousness, and that of the Planetary Body, then changing our enveloping environment Collectively into a higher state of being.

If the masses of humanity knew that a part of our anatomy allows us to alter our vibratory state, and our ability to commune with Spirit and access higher dimensions of reality, then I believe most World citizens would practice

these ancient Cosmic Kundalini
disciplines and access the God within
themselves, this then would lead them
to faith, which then leads to their
morality of being connected to others,
which leads to helping others around
them in their immediate communities,
instead of trying to just preserve
themselves through the lack of faith. So
World citizens need to start activating
their Kundalini oil fluids and anoint
themselves every month around the full
Moon, to preserve the Christ within,
with the understanding that the word
Christ means to be anointed with oil,
allowing us to activate our Christos
Angelic Human Light Body over a
period of dedicated time with this
focused attention on the Kundalini
energy rising into a fruit bering tree, to
allow us to become illuminated like
Christ, evolving into embodied Angelic
Human Beings of Light, once again in
our Eternal natural states of being,
connected to all in the Oneness of
Creation, the Brahaman, the Whole,

inside time and space in this Holographical Hyperdimensional light time Matrix of the three Primal Sound fields, and outside time and space in the Eternal realms, in the realms of Infinity. Where we join the ranks of the Luminous Ones, the Caretakers and Guardians of the Templar Sound field Hyperdimensional Light Time Matix of Geomancy, the animated form of all physical existence, created by the four fundamental forces of all animated life, that of electromagnetism, the weak and strong nuclear forces, and gravity the energy of Spirit, the energy of the Oneness Source field Collective Consciousness, that of Ultra Violet Divine energetic Consciousness. And when that Ultra Violet Source Consciousness is individual as a single Soul, it only weighs twenty one grams, when we are not embodied. We are the Yanas Ascened Masters, and Founder Races, and Souls from the Christos Collectives from the Interdimensional Association of Free Worlds, manifesting directly down into these lower dimensions onto this Planet Gaia, to effect emergency intervention on the Planet to free humanity from the domination and tyranny of other negatiative races and their human conspiritors, by teaching them to raise their Consciousness to activate their Eternal Light Body's, so they can ascend and transcend, returning to a natural embodied Eternal state of being.

Raising The Chrism: Santa Claus, Joseph Mary, and the Crucifiction.

1. The Pineal Gland 'Joseph' secrets the milk, the Pituitary 'Mary' secrets the honey, both from the same source the Claustrum 'Santa Claus'.

RAISING THE CHRISM: SANTA CLAUS JOSEPH MARY AND THE CRUCIFICTION

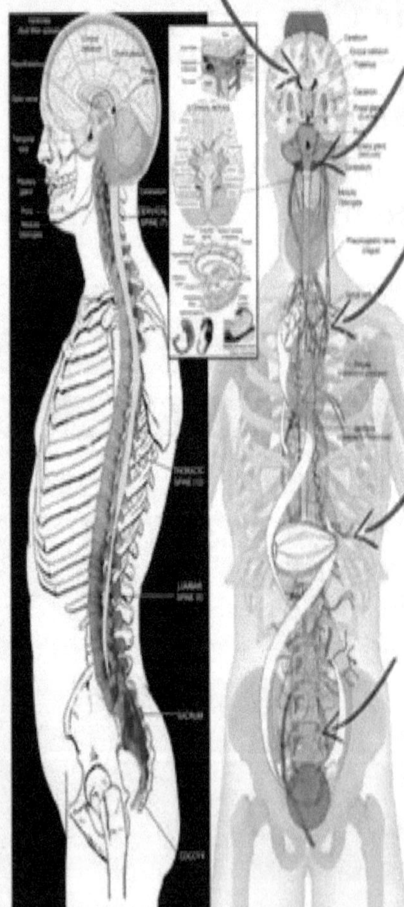

5. The sacred oilr returns after the crossing 'the crucifiction' it enters the cerebellum 'Golgotha' the place of the skull. The fluid 'Christ'is refined 1000 x fold.

2. The two sacred oils travel down into the solar plexus via the semi-lunar ganglion Pneumogastric nerve

3. The Psycho-Physical Germ 'the Fruit of the Tree of Life' is born in the Solar Plexus 'the Manger'

4. The Ida (red), Pingala (blue), two nervw fluids where at the crossing of the medulla oblongata the crucifiction takes place where it rests for 2 and a half days.

BUILDING KUNDALINI ENERGY

When meditating and breathing in sequence, you learn to squeeze at your base were the Kundalini gland resides, pulsating the gland with breath sequence, pulling energy upwards to the head, to the Pineal gland you be, Kundalini energy awakens and starts to rise, so you become a magnet and can pulse electromagnetic energy outwards, to manifest what you need in your life, pulsing electromagnetic energy waves outwards massively increases the intent of the matter you are creating, manifesting into being, like a magnet you attract the Creation of matter you manifested at speed.

So then the breath state sequence allows your Pineal gland to oscillate and then you can pick up signals beyond your normal senses, then the Pineal gland becomes a radio receiver, capable of transducing those frequencies that carry vital information into meaningful imagery, information imagery, the Sacred Geometric language of the Universe, visionary in nature, part of the Universal telepathy language you will see, this imagery information able to be accessed by all, to evolve and express yourself in your Universal unfolding.

CHAPTER FOUR

How To Fully Activate Your Pineal Gland Chakra Antennas

This information came from the Mayan culture, but many other shamanic tribal societies also knew this ancient knowledge and wisdom about the physics and quantum mechanics of the pineal gland at the center of the human brain, and that its light rod antennas had to also be activated. These pineal gland of rods can be called beams of light, this knowledge has been hidden and been kept secret, but the Mayans and other Shamanic tribal culture have always activated their own children's pineal gland and its light rod antennas. But as we know society has put a lot of fear into humanities children about psychic abilities, many of these fears are projected by the surrounding adults who are programmed to think it is demonic to have these abilities especially when it comes to telepathy, telekinesis, and levitation. And the adults project that onto their children and so the children switch off their psychic abilities which are then lost, because they are not practicing the disciplines needed to active the psychic abilities. Then we also have other forces like the negative exteraterrestrials that are suppressing humanity, that don't want us to access our extremely powerful divine gifts and psychic powers, because then they cant control and dominate humanity through the subconscious mind, and via mind control and through frequency technologies. Then we also have the Worlds militaries that are watching and looking for for children with psychic abilities for there secret military programs and for the secret space program. When we look back through human history we can clearly see that many beings that manifested in many cultures showed these types of gifts and psychic powers, many of them saints, prophets, and guru's. But at the core of the message of all of their teachings was if you find and connect with the light you can enter the kingdom of heaven, which translates to if you raise your body's vibrational frequency and raise your consciousness, you can access your eternal human light body and transcend the Creation and enter the eternal realms. These teachers also gave permission to use these psychic abilities within their teachings of coming back to the heart and moving away from the mind, allowing you access to all possibilities of the angelic human lineages potential, if its software field the luminous energy schematic blueprint is reinformed to then activate the full twelve strands of DNA, which is the hardware that creates the manifested physical human avatar temple.

Also the pineal gland chakra light rod antennas are exactly the same as your breathing tube, they are a straight fluoresent tube.

Below Is An Image Of The Fully Activated Pineal Gland Chakra Antennas That Create The Angelic Human Halo

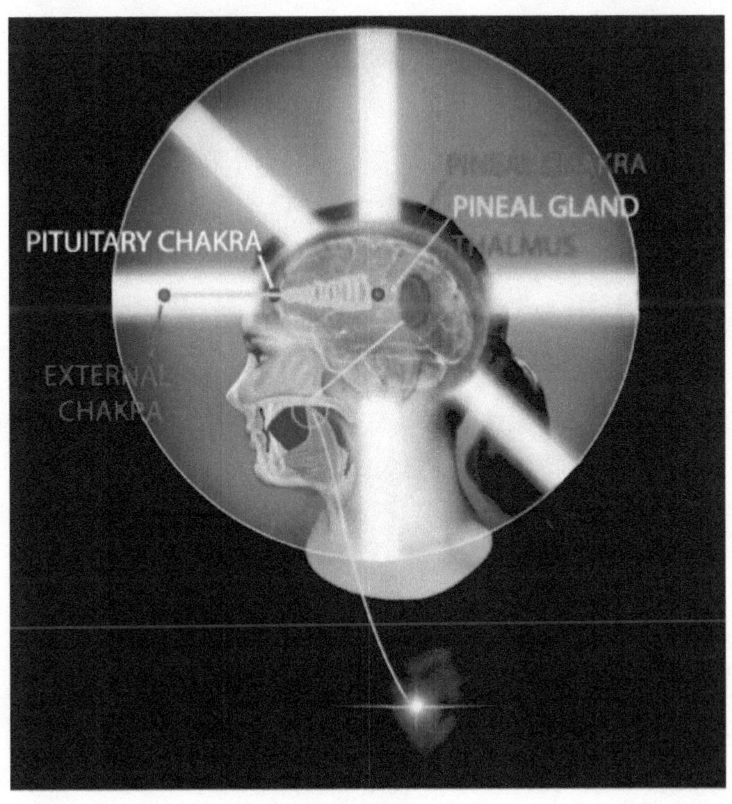

Diagram of head with fuzzy floppy bent pineal light rods after not being used & activated for thousands of years

But the pineal gland tubes don't look straight when they are coming out of the skull the head, because they have been deactivated for thousands of

years, but with work and practice they can be reactivated and straightened out back into the straight light rods beams that are connected to the pineal gland chakra.

Diagram of head facing left with straight pineal light rod beams activated

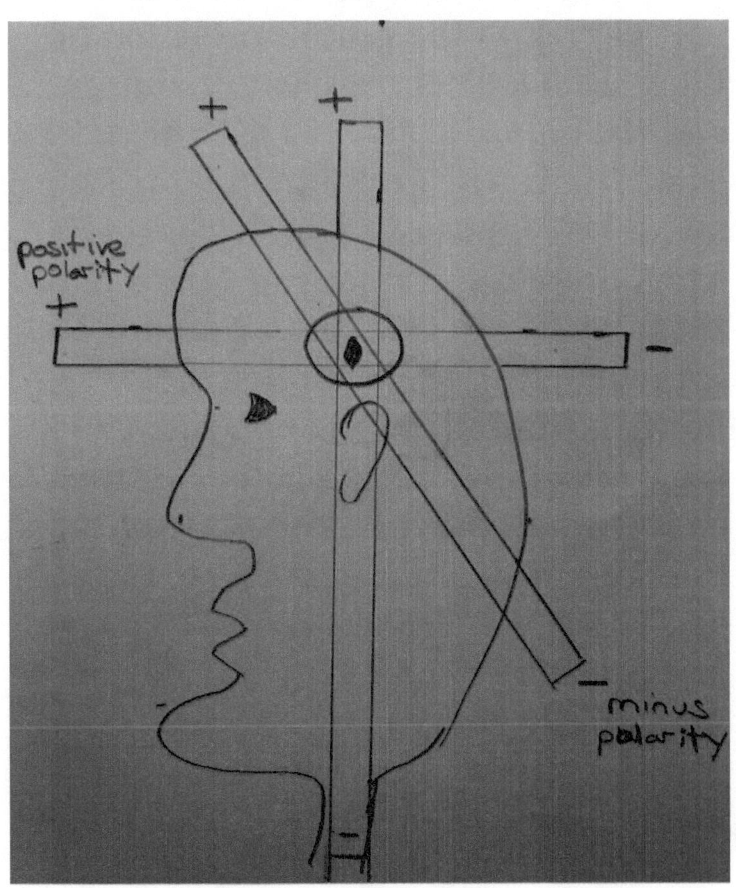

So there are eight light rods in total, one through the third eye that's horizontal that protrudes out of the third eye at the front of the head which is of positive charge, the other end of that rod it protrudes out of the back of the head that is another light rod that is the negative charge, then there is on vertical out of the center of the top of the skull which is the positive charge and the opposite end of the light rod comes down the neck into the throat and is the opposite negative charge. Then there is one light rod that is on the forty five degree angle out of the front center of the head this the positive charge and the opposite end at the back of lower head is the negative charge, then the final two come out of the sides of the head just above the ears on the left side it is the positive charge and the light rod on the right side of the head is the negative charge.

Diagram of head at 3D angle showing all pineal rods activated & polarity of positive & negative charge

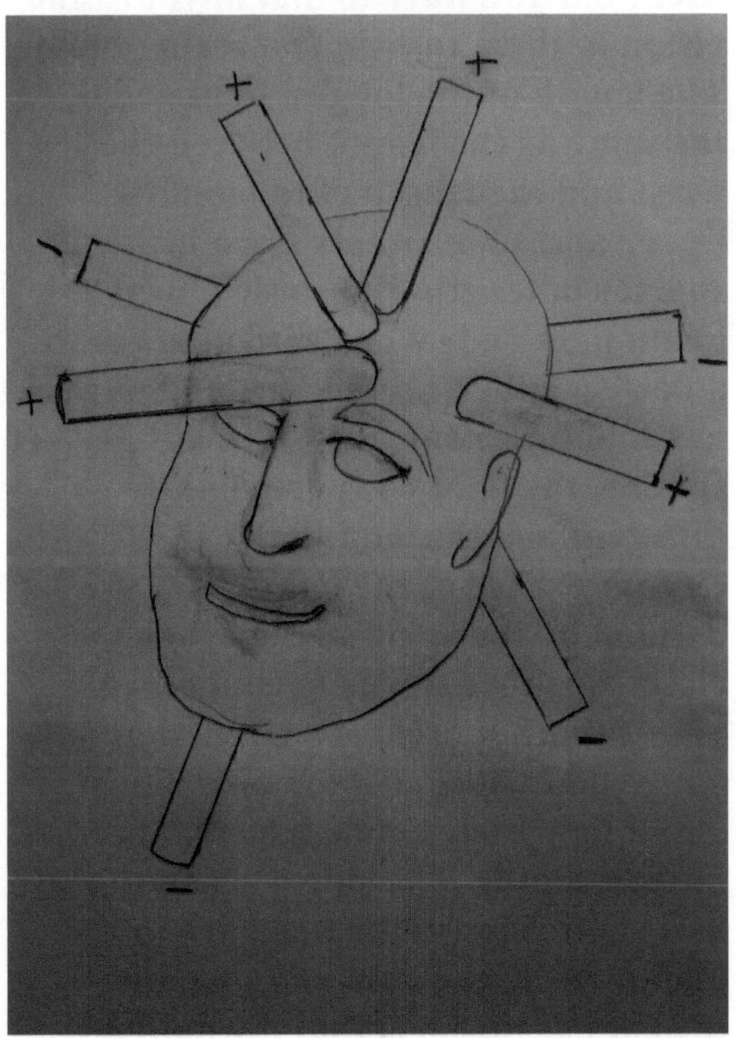

So you can see from the images what they look like and its said that when you can perceive and see them that they are brighter than the aura field itself, but you have to dial in your inner vision to them to manifest seeing them. The length of the longest light rod is the same as the length between the wrist and the length of the middle finger and some others are a little bit shorter in length. But these pineal gland light rods when activated create a perfect spherical field around our head, because our heads are not perfect spheres the light rods are slightly different lengths, and the circumference of the light rodes are defined by the same size as when you close your fore finger to connect to your thumb it creates a circle that's the gauge and width of your own pineal gland light rodes, it depends on the size of your hands. The side rods on the left and right sides of the head are in alignment of the ears and just above the ears at the level that it would go straight through the pineal gland, but it does not through the pineal gland it connects to the pineal gland chakra as do all of the pineal gland light rods. So these rods are antenna that receive images from the heart, this is the link to the heart and the brain, and if they are not functioning then you do not have a connection between the heart and the brain. The truth is all ancient texts say there was a great fall, and you can perceive that as a fall through the consciousness dimensional levels, or substantially a much simpler basic way of saying it is that we were in the past living in our heart space and manifesting from there, then the fall happened in consciousness and we moved into the brain. So the true definition of ascension is basically moving back into the heart space, so that we can manifest with clarity at a higher frequency range, its that simple. And the idea's of when we think of the other parallel Worlds and other dimensions is only more mental stuff that is absolutely associated with an external mind function. We have to remember that we have the genetic schematic blueprints of divine eternal angelic human beings, the genetics of goddesses and gods, so we can manifest and create any encompassing reality that we wish to experience, in this dimension and in the higher dimensions. And because this information has been held back and hidden from humanity, we as a consciousness collective, as an entire race have been operating at the subconscious level and operating unconsciously in a disorderly fashion. We are not directing and driving our consciousness, which has lead us to manifest a much more chaotic encompassing reality to live in, but I must say the negative extraterrestials and their genetic manipulation on humanity and the negative technologies that they use on us are all apart of the suppression of humanities consciousness individually and as a collective, by manipulating our subconscious minds.

Image of the activated Golden Crown
The Human Diamond Halo

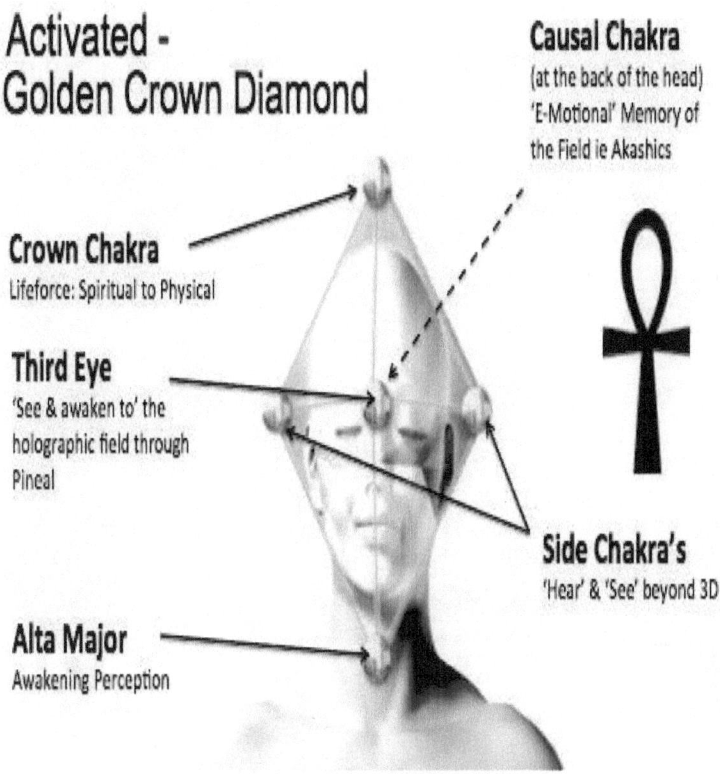

Now going back to the pineal gland light rod beams, there is a particular order that they have to be activated,

because when you reconstruct them they must be reconnected in order in sets, because they also have a polarity associated to them.

Diagram of the specific numbered order to activated pineal light rods

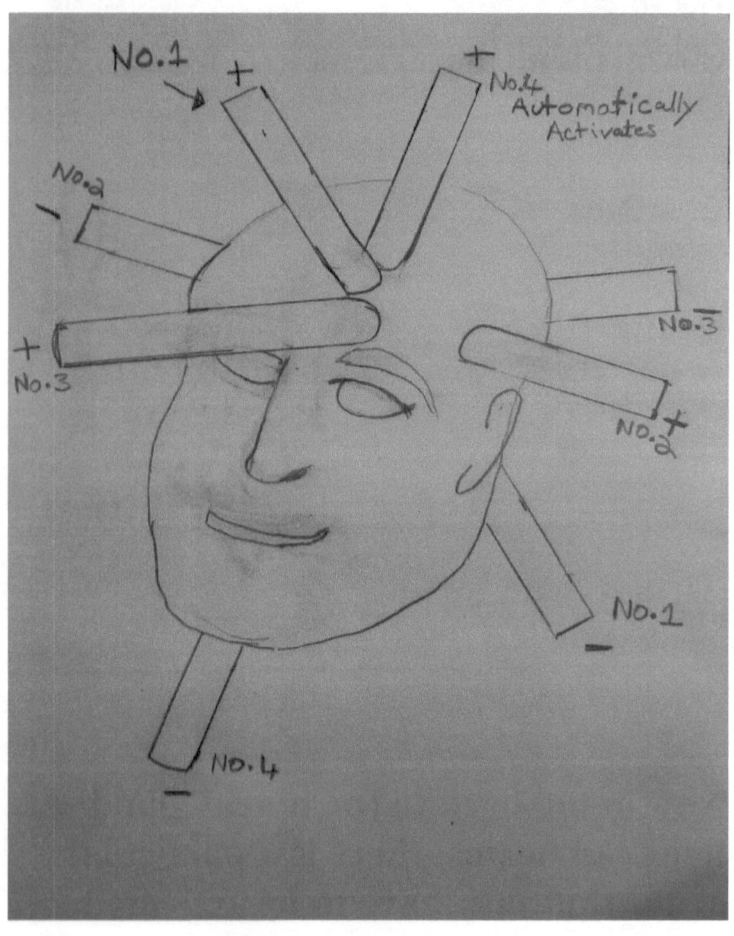

When the pineal gland light rod beams light up it is because they are connected to the pineal gland chakra, and the beams of light all shoot out from the center of the pineal gland chakra to protrude out of the head, but there is also a flow coming into the negative polarity rods and the light comes in the rod and enters and moves in a spiralling fashion because its rotating, just as the same with our own breathing tubes the light is coming down in a spiral fashion rotating one way and coming back up rotating the other direction, like are Mer-Ka-Ba field its two vortexes into vortex field rotating in each opposite direction. So all of the light entering and exiting the pineal gland light filament rods are spiralling as they create the beams of light protruding from the shull from the head. Then the heart is completely linked back to the brain the way it was before the great fall around thirteen thousand years ago, before genetic manipulation and intrusion by negative forces with negative agenda's.

When you actually understand the mechanics and physics of the pineal gland light rod beams its no very hard to activate them, you'll be surprised with a little bit of discipline and daily dedication to the visualization process and feeling your encompassed by these reactivated pineal gland rods, you can active them very quickly, because once you set up and activate one light rod beam antenna its then easy to activate the remaing pineal light rods, by repeating the same process over and over again until all pineal gland rods are activated, and it is absolutally much easier to activate them quicker than it is at activating your Mer-Ka-Ba field, your human light body.

So now lets look at what will happen inside the head, the skull, inside the brain, as the light in a rod leaves the surface of the skull, the beams are projecting pure white clean beams of light. But where the rods leave the skull from the inside of the skull there are these strands that are curved and fluctuate always moving on a continuum, they resonate very organically moving and lighting up as they move to the center of the brain (these strands move like you see in a Plasma Ball or Globe with Lightening Effect, they are used for education & science, they create an electrical plasma field and when you place your hand on the Globe the strands of Plasma energy moves towards your hands, this is what these electric strands look like moving from the skull inwards) towards the center of the head, towards the pineal chakra, then the strand reconnect to the pineal chakra. The next two diagrams shows the mechanics of this process.

Diagram of electrical light strands connected from skull to pineal chakra

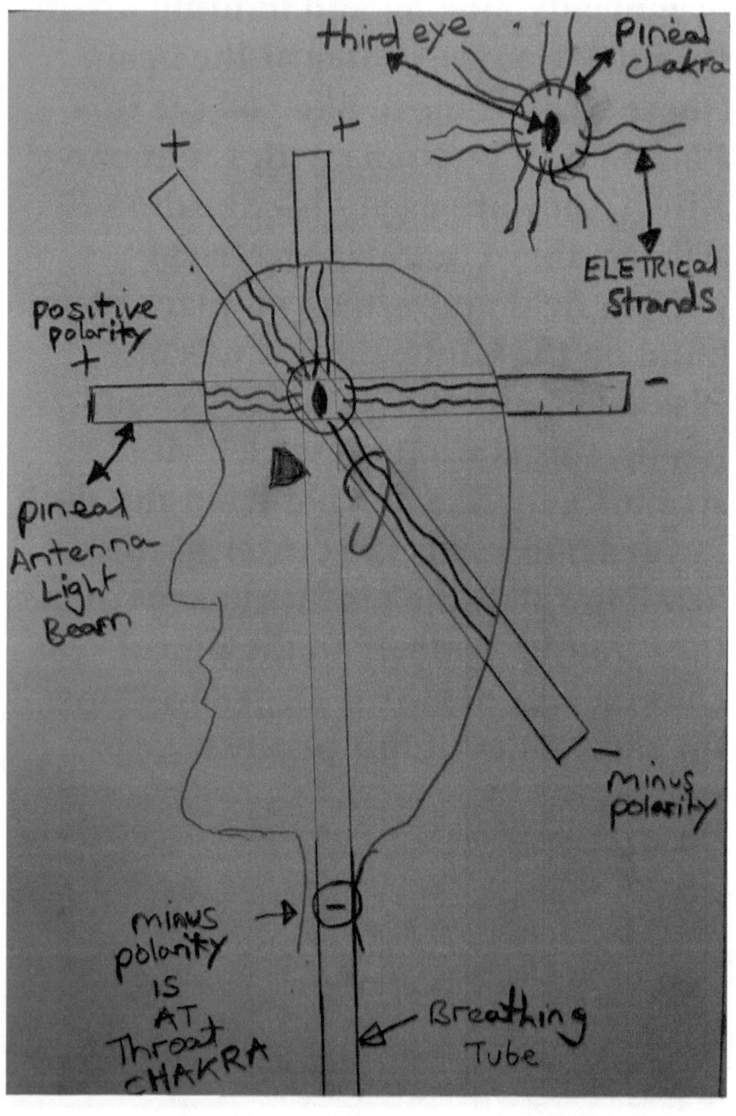

So when these pineal gland rods are activated and the light strands of electricity are actively moving this means that you are completely connected to the heart, to the heart space, to the heart chakra.
But for most people with their pineal gland light rods not activated this is just not the case because when we look at the following diagram below we can see inside the skull and brain, and instead these electrical fluxing light strands come from the skull and have no direction, they go no where not connecting as they should, they seem to avoid the pineal gland area and its chakra, it does not connect. Many have had theories why they don't connect and why this took place at a certain point in our history, but even some teachers of this knowledge are not totally sure they can only speculate to the possibilities of several theories, but it was the knave Anunnaki's fractal manipulation of the blueprint design of the angelic human schematics.

Diagram of head with pineal antenna electrical strands as floppy misshaped light strands not connecting to centre pineal gland chakra

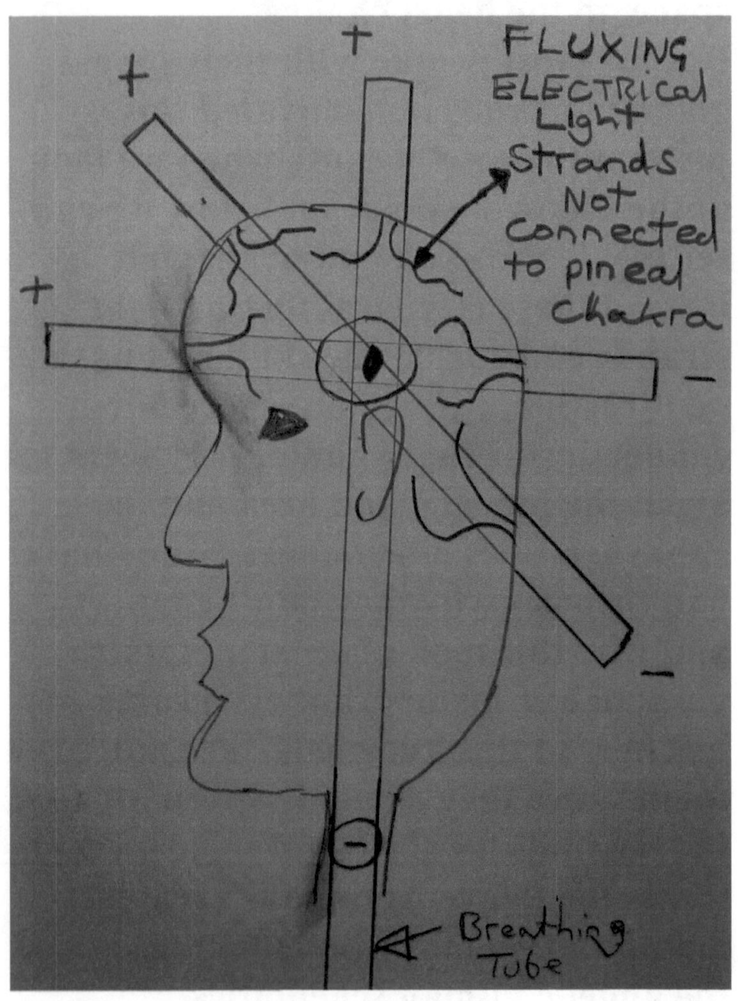

It has also been discovered that most children, even eighty percent of psychically gifted children, reaching teenage puberty, that they start to grown a calcium shield around the pineal gland, you can perceive this like an oyster shell around the pineal gland. This blocks the connection to the electromagnetic field around us in our encompassing environment, stopping our connection to the Universe and our psychic communication with our Star families from previous incarnations. This is the same calcium that causes arthritis pain, this is because bad calcium that come from milk and dairy products build up and create arthritis in the joints of the body, it also builds up in the ears causing deafness, and builds up in the eyes causing bad eye sight or even blindness. So this oyster calcium shell like sheild around the pineal gland just blocks our psychic abilities, and stops us accessing our other ten stands of DNA, to access our Mer-Ba-Ka field. The ordinary unconscious individuals in society have calcification through out many parts of their body's, so their pineal glands are not activated, neither are their pineal gland light rod beams activated, and the resonating electrical light strands from the rods inside the skull are not moving in the correct fashion towards conneting to the pineal gland chakra. The calcium seals around the pineal gland but it is the pineal chakra that the strands connect to and work off of, so the fluxing electrical strands connect only to th pineal chakra not to the pineal gland.

So what World citizens need to do now is reconnect and straighten their pineal gland light rod antenna's and activate the fluxing electrical strands to connect to the pineal chakra, to have it fully activated. And stop putting bad dairy calcium in their body's and ingest fulvic acid drops daily and MSM (Methylsulfonylmethan) to break down the calcium in the body and around the pineal gland. You can also take Zeolite daily that removes heavy metals from the body. So if you reconnect the pineal light rods you will have the potential of reconnecting to your heart space, to your heart chakra, so you can manifest from the heart. So when we come to the physics of this subject the pineal gland is the source of power, its like the heart is on the of left side of the chest and the heart chakra is in the centre of the chest, and they are both very different and important and there is a connection between them both, because the heart is the source of the heart chakra, and there are some things you will do or access with the heart chakra, and there are some other things you do or access with the heart. Then when we perceive all of our luminous energy field systems and light body systems, we see they are all interconnected, like the Leonardo da Vinci sphere our luminous energy field that's connected to to our pineal gland light beams, to our light sphere around our head that is intimately connected six inches above the head via the crown chakra to the Mer-Ka-Ba field as it expands around us encompassing our physical body, there is a very direct relationship between the two. They are both directly connected to the crown chakra outside of the body above the head about six inches, so there is a direct linked connection between the two. Leonardo da Vinci is famous for his illustration of the man inside the sphere because it depicts the human luminous energy field that surrounds and envolopes our physical body, which is our personal energetic space, it is perceived as a translucent multi-coloured rainbow bubble of light energy. The next image is of the translucent human energy field depicted by Leonardo da Vinci.

The Leonardo da Vinci sphere
known as The Vitruvian Man depicting
the Human Luminous Energy Field

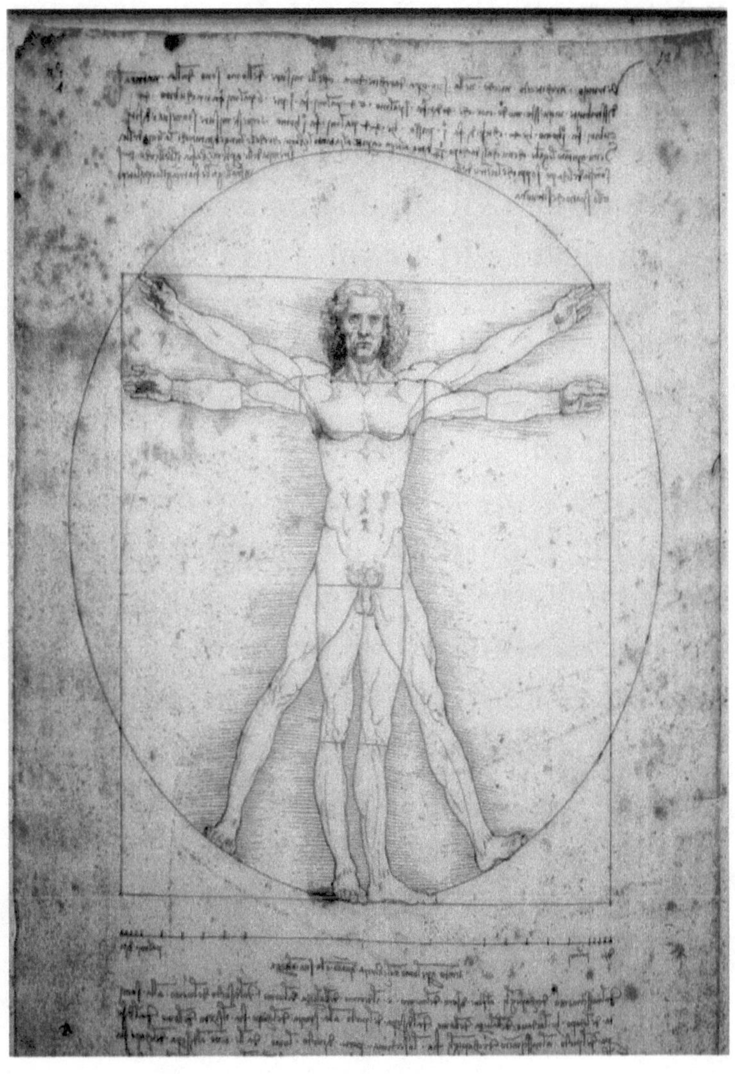

So these are the Mayan teachings of the instructions to access and reactivate your pineal rod light filament beams. Now the Mayans teachings are how to work on another person, this is because they teach you how they do this to their children when they activate their pineal light filament rods, but you can apply this to yourself to activate your own pineal light beams. So you start at the front of the head on number one rod which is the diagonal rod of positive polarity, to get its correct location on the head take your thumb touching your chin and your forefinger touching the tip of your nose, hold that distance between your thumb and forefinger and put your thumb touching the tip of your nose and where your forefinger touches your forehead is where the third eye horizontal light beams location resides, then you do the same again move your thumb to your third eye light rod location and your forefinger above will give you the location of your diagonal light rod. And if you do the same again by placing your thumb on the diagonal light beam location then your forefinger will give you the location on the top of your head where the vertical light beam is positioned. So this is the procedure to activate them on another person by them facing to your left side and you standing by their left sholder side, it has to be done like this on the left side of body because you cant stand on the right side of their body if your working on someone else because it wont work. The reason it wont work is because the number one diagonal light rod has a positive charge and its opposite end out the of the skull is a negative charge, and you are using your hands to activate the rods and your left hand has a negative charge and your right hand has a positive charge. So when you use your hands to couple over the top of these rods the left negative hand will couple with the front diagonal rod and the right positive hand will couple the back

diagonal beam at the lower back of the head. This then creates the correct positive and negative current flows of energy to activate the pineal rods light beams.

Image of hands cupping positive and negative diagonal charge rods

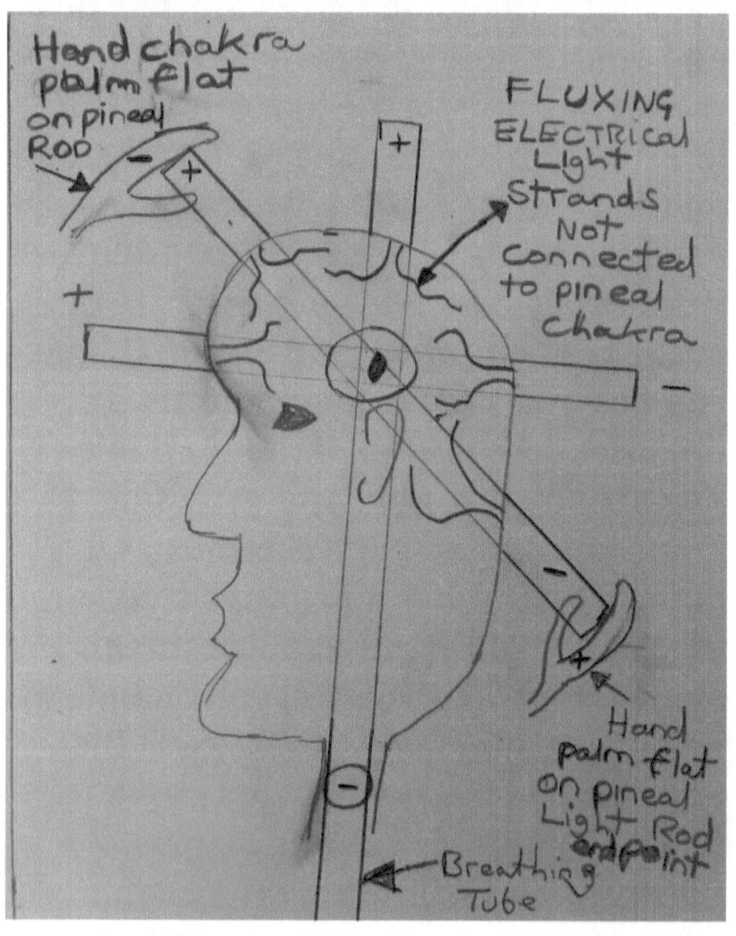

So you visualize the light beams with focused intention and hold onto the front and back diagonal light beams and pull outwards at the same time. You communicate to the other persons body or your own body with intention but you don't have to speak out loud you can speak in your own mind with focused intention and the other persons body or your own will hear your communication, and then with intention direct the shrivelled bent pineal rods to stretch out and go into a beam of light, and they will do so instantly but they will only be short length beams to start with, maybe an inch long to start with until the power from the heart chakra flows stronger, which will then extend them longer in length, with full power activated from the heart chakra they will extend to full length pineal rod light beams. So you hold the two diagonal rods like you hold the handle bars on a bike and start with intention to go into a beam of light, but they will be very short and you will sense which one is stronger in energy and then you start with the weaker one which is usually the diagonal negative charge one at the back of the head, and you communicate to just that one with intention to flow with more energy and to extend its length longer. The pineal rod will extend longer but very little to start with because the body has not done this for thousands of years, so a long time, so you keep the intention to pull much more energy from the pineal chakra, but you don't extend it any further outwards than the palm width of your hand, you can now focus attention on making it wider to one inch, this will allow it to output a lot more energy, so you keep telling it to output more energy until it gets wider and stronger in energy flow until it is the length of the width of the palm of your hand then communicate intention to stop. Then you switch rods and start working on the more powerful front diagonal pineal rod and repeat the same process while holding both the front and back rods at the same time, you will have to communicate intention and repeat this around ten times to extend the rods and activate the heart chakra power through the pineal rods. Then the next stage in this process to to move your hands away from the rods and then place your hands with palms open so that your hand chakras are exposed, and place them over the ends of the two diagonal rod beam points, with your left negative hand on the front of the head and right positive hand at the lower back of the head. It's the same when you are activating your own pineal light beams you place left hand on your forehead and your right hand on the back of your own head, but you can also do this to yourself without using your hands, you can be just sitting in lotus position with hands touching for the energy flow, and use your intention, visualization, and use your feeling of them strengthening and activating, because you are communicating to your own fields of your body so it is very clear communication, but some people are more comfortable and need to feel by touching and placing their hands in the pineal rod locations on the head. So when you have your hand chakras over the points of the diagonal rods the next thing you do is close your eyes and perceive and see inside the body with your eyes closed and with your focused attention you look to see the pineal chakra, and for most people it appears as red in colour, in others it appears as the colour black, or it can also be seen as turquoise in colour, it depends on the individual. The next thing to do in this process is to focus on both diagonal rod beams and vizulize the fluxing light strands from the inside of skull where the rod pretudes from the skull, and visually see the strands activating from the rod at the skull and connecting to the pineal chakra in the center of the head. It takes a lot of visual intended focus on the electrical light strands to get them to connect because its been so long since they have been connected and activated, they appear to move away at first like they are opposite polarity's but with persistence the strands will reconnect and stay connected. But you have to keep them connected for one to two minutes depending on the individual, and keep them connected until you can perceive and feel that they will not detach apart. Then with your focused attention from the center of the pineal chakra you pull both of the beams of light outwards down along their length to the end points of both diagonal light beams external end points out past the sphere of light that they create, because they will stop at the right length externally by themselves. The light from the center of the pineal chakra will with your intention directly follow your hand chakras and allow the flow of light down the rods as you move your hands outwards to the ends of the pineal rods. The next stage is to focus your intention on the very end points of the two diagonal pineal rods, and you will be able to perceive that they are vibrating in a pulsing fashion, you should feel this pulsing through your hand chakras in the palms of your hands. So at first they are not vibrating and pulsing the same, so with your intention you have to get them to vibrate at the same rate of pulse, visualizing and repeating in your mind for them to vibrate at the same pulsating resonance. At first the two pulses will be out of synchronization and slow, then they will get quicker and chaotic, then they will just click and the two end points of the diagonal pineal rods will vibrate at the right speed and resonance, at the right pulsing rate in sync with one another. And as soon as they sync you start counting the pulses until you get to a minimum of twenty pulses to stabalize and activate the two diagonal pineal rod beams of light. Then you can remove both of your hands from the

head and and the light strands and pineal light beams will stay there in place fully connected.

Diagram of rod antenna with fluxing light strands from the skull to the heart chakra

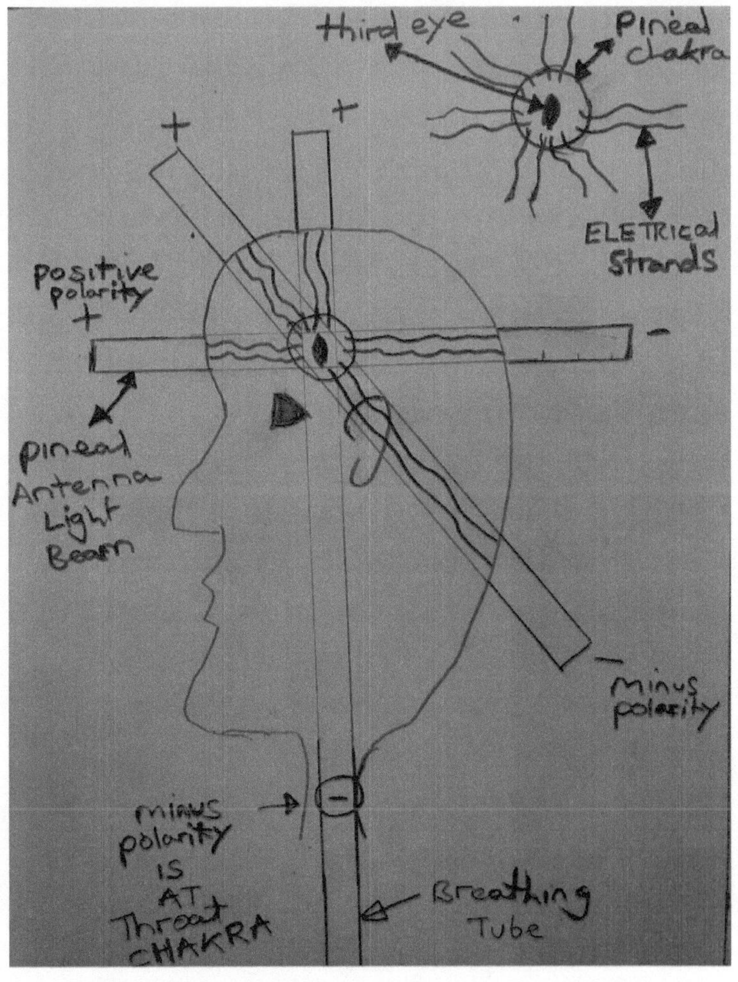

Then the next stage to connect the next
pineal rods in the process is to move
your position and stand behind the
person to activate the number two
pineal gland rods which is the side rods
on the left and right side of the head,
not at the temple area, they are
actually located just above the ears. So
you are standing behind the person
and you just repeat the same stages of
the process you did to activate your
first two diagonal pineal light rod
beams. Remember you started with the
fuzzy bent light beams and if they are
slightly out of position you pull them
back into the correct position with
your visual focused intention, then feel
which one is the weaker one and
communicate with the body and get the
weaker pineal rod to extend straight
outwards, then extend the stronger
pineal rod outwards, then place your
two hand palm chakras over the end
points of the pineal rods, and perceive
inside the head with your eyes closed
and visually see the fluxing electrical

light strands and the pineal chakra and visualize and feel them reconnect and hold the connection for one to two minutes to be sure there connected. Once they are connected then you pull the beams of light outwards from the center of the pineal chakra along the length of the pineal rods outwards until they are protruding out of the head say one foot. Then you use your hand chakras by placing your palms on the end points of the side pineal rods, and atune and feel the pulsing, and focus your intention to resonate them both at the same frequency, at the same pulsating resonance in sync together. And as soon as they are in sync you start counting the pulses until you get to a minimum of twenty pulses to stabalize and activate the two side pineal rod beams of light. Then you can remove both of your hands from the head and the light strands and the pineal light beams will stay there in place fully connected.

Diagram of standing behind a person activating set No.2 pineal rods with palms on side pineal rods

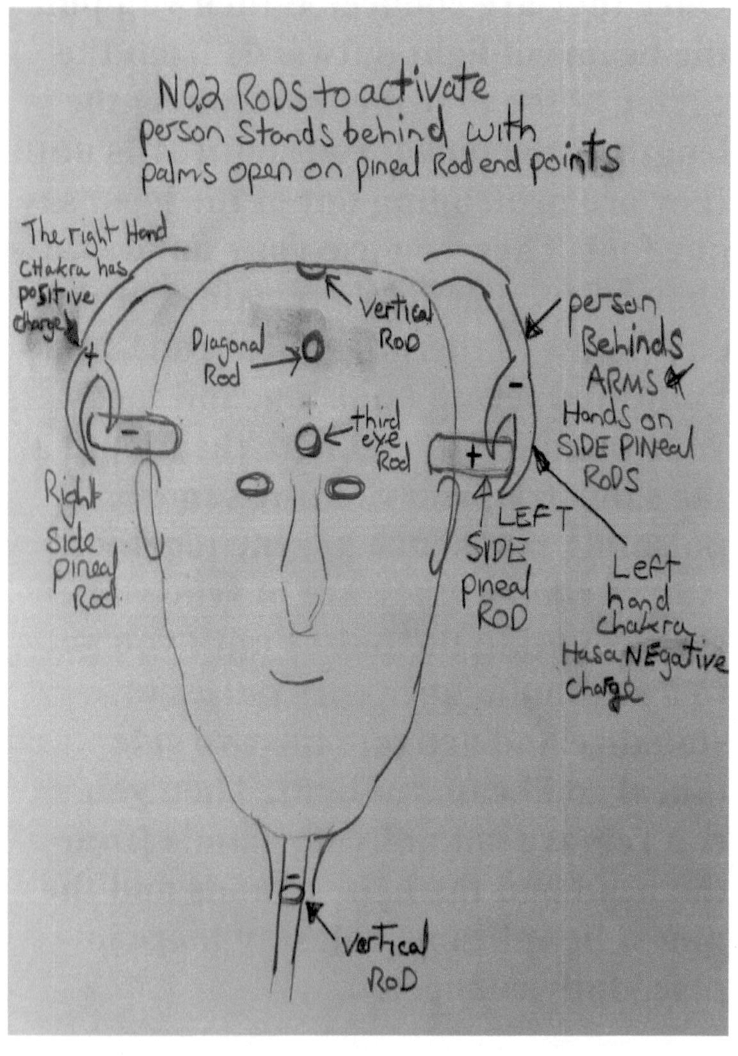

Then the next stage in the process is to then come to the position of your third eye pineal rod set at the front of the head and work on that one and the other horizontal one at the back of the head, by repeating the whole process again until those two pineal rods are activated with a steady continuous beam of light powered by energy from the pineal chakra. Then the vertical pineal rods above and below your head will then naturally activate themselves atomatically. But if there was a problem with the vertical one it's a bit awkward to activate because you have to put your left hand on the top of the vertical pineal rod position and you would use your right hand below at the perineum location point. But you can only reach the lower vertical rod position from an even lower position, from the location of the perineum, which is located between the anus and scotum or vulva in humans. There is no other way because it is located a long way up the breathing tube from the

perineum to the position of the pineal
rod which is located in the centre of
your throat. But this is extremely rare
for your vertical pineal rods not to
activate automatically after the others
have already been activated.

So once the pineal rod light beams are
operating, when you are working on
another person they will usually shut
off and collapse after about fifteen
minutes of being activated, and then
you will have to start at the beginning
of the process and go all the way
through the stages until all of the
pineal rod light beams have been
reactivated, and most of the time the
second full process of activating them
will hold and stay activated. But if they
do not then do all the stages of the
whole process again for a third time
and they will be fully activated. And to
keep them permentaly activated you
will need to do this activation sequence
daily for two weeks then they should be
permentaly stable, and then your light
sphere halo around your head will be

activated and stable, and as long as you stay connected in the heart space, it should be operating on a continuum. So once the pineal rods are operating it wont do a lot of function even though its running, because it's the same as the Mer-Ka-Ba field not doing to much when its running, until all light fields are lined up into one united connected light field. Then you will access your full eternal divine angelic human light body.

Now lets go back to the standard time frame of activating a childs pineal rod light beam, that is when they reach the age of puberty entering their teenage years. And a lot of these psychic children are consciously pulling light energy into their forth and fifth lumbar region situated in the back between the lowest ribs and the pelvis, then they pull that light energy horizontal inwards to their core center and then turn it ninty degrees into the vertical direction, then they send it directly upwards through their spine, through their core center. With this type of light activation work on our chakras, antennas, and luminous fields, around the World there has been many blind people that have been trained in activating and operating their pineal gland to percieve their encompassing physical reality that surrounds them, and also talt to read and write, and to drive a vehicle and watch television. Many blind people are actually functioning consciously outside of their physical body's and are even consciously operating by floating around in the Solar System by using their activated internal third eye.

So now going back to when you are doing your work of focused attention of visualization and feeling on another person, you are seeing inside your minds eye and perceiving inside the head of the other persons mechanics of the pineal rods, the pineal chakra, and the fluxing electrical light strands, so you are either seeing, sensing, or feeling when you are doing this work, and be clear and use your intuition and your intention, because intention is everything, just to be clear on that part of the process.

So now going back to the sequence of activating the pineal light beams and activating your own pineal light beams on yourself, you have to start with pineal beam number one which the diagonal beam, then you do number two beam next which is on the left and right side of tha head, then you do number three next which is the horizontal beam at the third eye level of the head, and number four the vertical beam you do not have to activate because it opens automatically. It also good to know that your pineal gland is the same size as your eyes but is more circular in shape, and don't forget the pineal gland is literally scientifically an eye of vision, and the third eye is hollow with colour receptors inside of it and there is a lense on it for perceiving light. But because it has not been activated and used for thousands of years it has shriveled down to the size of a pea, but with continued focused work on the gland and by using it, it will start to grow back just like a muscle does with more active use of the muscle it strengthen and grows back bigger and stronger, it's the same for the third eye. Also the lense of the eye is looking upwards out of the tube at the top centre of the head, and it is designed to perceive light from above. So the pineal gland is literally a functioning eye ball but it also has many other functions. And its been proven that when light comes into the pineal gland eye from above it then sends it literally directly to every single cell in the body, this means every single cell of your body can then see everything you are perceiving and looking at, because that light information is saturated into every single cell of your body.

Then when your pineal rods are activated and your light sphere halo is continually operating, the halo then becomes the link to your Mer-Ka-Ba body, the link to your eternal human light body, which is sixy foot light field sphere encompassing and enveloping the physical body. The Mer-Ka-Ba light field is a perfect sphere, and there is also a disc like shape that operates and runs through it, because the link between the outer light body and the inner creation process of the heart is operating through the pineal complex of interwoven and interconnected systems.

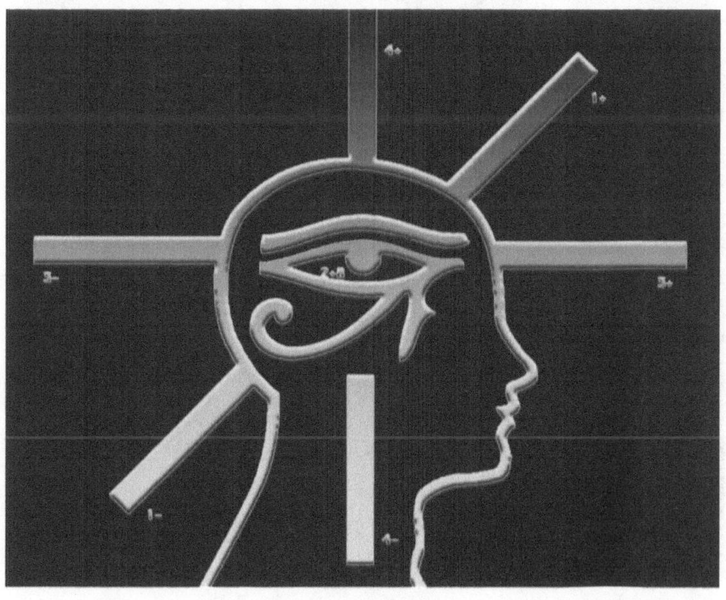

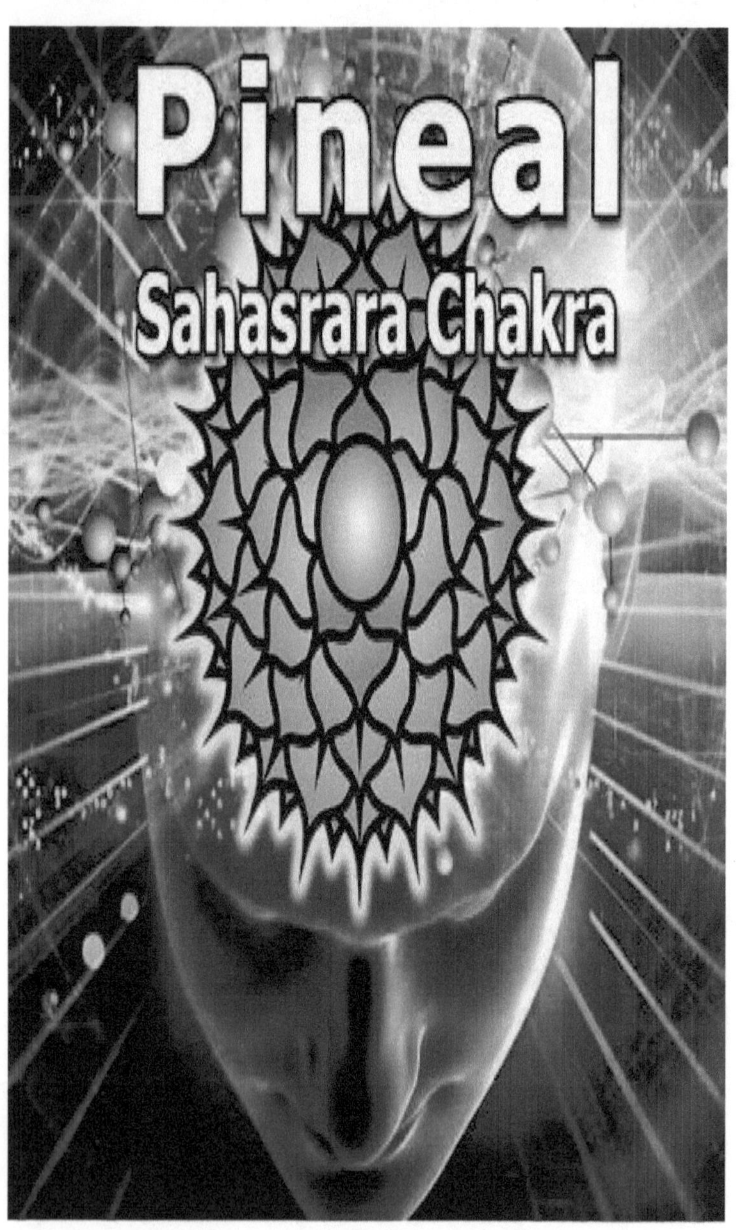

Pineal
Sahasrara Chakra

CHAPTER FIVE

The Heart The Beginning Of Life
The Link Between
Geometrics & The Heart

So the links between the heart and geometries operate and continue on every level which also includes conception. So when a human being is born they start out as a sphere, which is the perfect sphere of the ovum itself, then through mitosis, which is a part of the cell cycle in which replicated chromosomes are separated into two new nuclei. Cell division by mitosis, is an equational division which gives rise to genetically identical cells in which the total number of chromosomes is maintained. So through the mitosis process the human sphere itself divides into two, then divides from two to four, that's when it creates and forms an exact tetrahedron, then when it divides from four to eight it then forms a tetrahedron facing downwards in direction and one tetrahedron facing upwards, which is called a stsr tetrahedron, which is simultaneusly a cube. So it proceeds through these interconnected geometric relationships until it gets to five hundred and twelve cells, then it forms the torus field shape of an apple which is known as a toroidal field, which one of the original fields that came out of Creation. Then that toridal field continues to grow and becomes the human heart, and so there is a manifesting point in time that every human being has been through and that is that they were a only manifested as a heart at that point in time of evolving and nothing else, just a beating heart. It took scientists studying the heart some time to understand how the heart started beating because there was no intelligence that they were aware of, because there was no brain just the heart. Then it was discovered that there was a brain inside of the heart itself, and its make up is jusy forty thousand cells, so this is were the intelligence came from the heart itself. Then after a while the physical avatar the human body emerges from out of the heart, and then the heart is wrapped within the human body, then after that the second brain the gut and the third head brain is formed.

This is why ancient verbal teachings and texted scripture from ancient societies like the Vadas, and the native indigenous tribal cultures, say there is a direct central connected nature of the heart to human consciousness, because the heart is fundamentally more important than the head brain. In our human past ages there was a time that all human beings lived in their heart space, meaning their eternal spirit was centered and operated from inside of their heart, and they used their brain as a remote viewing perception instrument to perceive and see in the multidimensional reality fields of Creation. They used the head brain for that perception purpose because they were actually residing and living within their heart, within their heart space, and making their decisions from feeling from within the heart center, because they were heart based. So they were living a completely different way of life, to manifest their encompassing experiences of living life, and so their fundamental perceptions of life and its fundamental meaning, was completely different to how we perceive life today. You have to go back in in time in history when there was a great fall, which has been speculated to be around over twelve thousand years ago which many have also speculated that there were many different reasons for this and why it happened. From ancient knowledge pasted down the generations on the Planet about the great fall, it states that in that time frame there was a misuse of energy that caused humans to fall. Its been perceived in so many ways by many, but the great fall really in a physiological way of perceiving and looking at things, was the fall was simply that our spirit moved from the heart to the constructs of the mind, And so for thousands of years we have been living and manifesting from the brain rather than the heart. This caused the effect of what we know as ego, which is a part of us that only thinks of its self, and not so much about others. Once we are manifesting via living in the heart space, all the negative surrounding realities of war and poverty of our environment, all of these external manifestations will cease to exist.

But now is a new era for humanity a time of rapid evolution if we leave the mind and move our spirit to our hearts, then we step into the golden age, the fifth dimension of consciousness, and into the age of ascension and into all possibilities of timelines, like transcending space and time, and stepping into the eternal realms. And when we are living and manifesting from the heart space, we will look after each other and care and love one another, this is because its all about us connecting and uniting together and cooperating with each other, working in sync unifed. When humanity is in the heart and returns into balance with the Earths vibratory electromagnetic consciousness field, it will be easy for us to manifest a peaceful enveloping reality environment, and to resolve the issues we face making that change on the Planet and in society. For humanity to have the enveloping reality we currently are living in we left the heart and started manifesting from the mind, which is mad at best of times because its operated from ego. Then being in the mind we felt and were separated from each other and from our environment, and from the manifesting electromagnetic fields of the zero point energy fields of Creation. This duality reality separation experience makes humans feel that we are inside of our body/s and whats outside of our body's is not connected to us. This is not true and is not the case at all because that is the illusion, because when humans are back in their heart space you would know that everything is interconnected to the Creations oneness field. Then with that full conscioue awareness we know that if we hurt or harm another person mentally, as in verbally, or emotionally, or physically, that we would then instantly feel the pain we gave to another, because we would understand that hurting another is hurting ourselves. But now at this time in this three dimensional reality and state of separated consciousness it is not apparent to us in this lower state of awareness how interconnected we truly are because we are in the brain in the mind. And so we cannot see, feel, or sense, or perceive these other connected fields around us with our limited sense of sight, touch, and feeling, we just cannot perceive the interconnected oneness fields of Creation. These are the intimate interconnected electromagnetic fields of the holographical hyperdimensional light time templar matrix of Creation, that intimately connect all life every where in the whole Creation, that is also known as the Oneness field. The human race needs to wake up and remember that we need to live in the heart, then we can once again perceive that there are so many variable possibilities of manifesting and living life, we have to come into awareness to understand we have not had the awareness of all the other possible ways of existing and being that are amazing, wonderous, and absolutely awesome, just majestically astonishing and marvellous. Because we will step away from the lower state of fear based consciousness into higher states of consciousness, into abundance, joy, laughter, fun, and it will be a pleasure manifesting and living in states of contentment, satisfaction, and bliss.

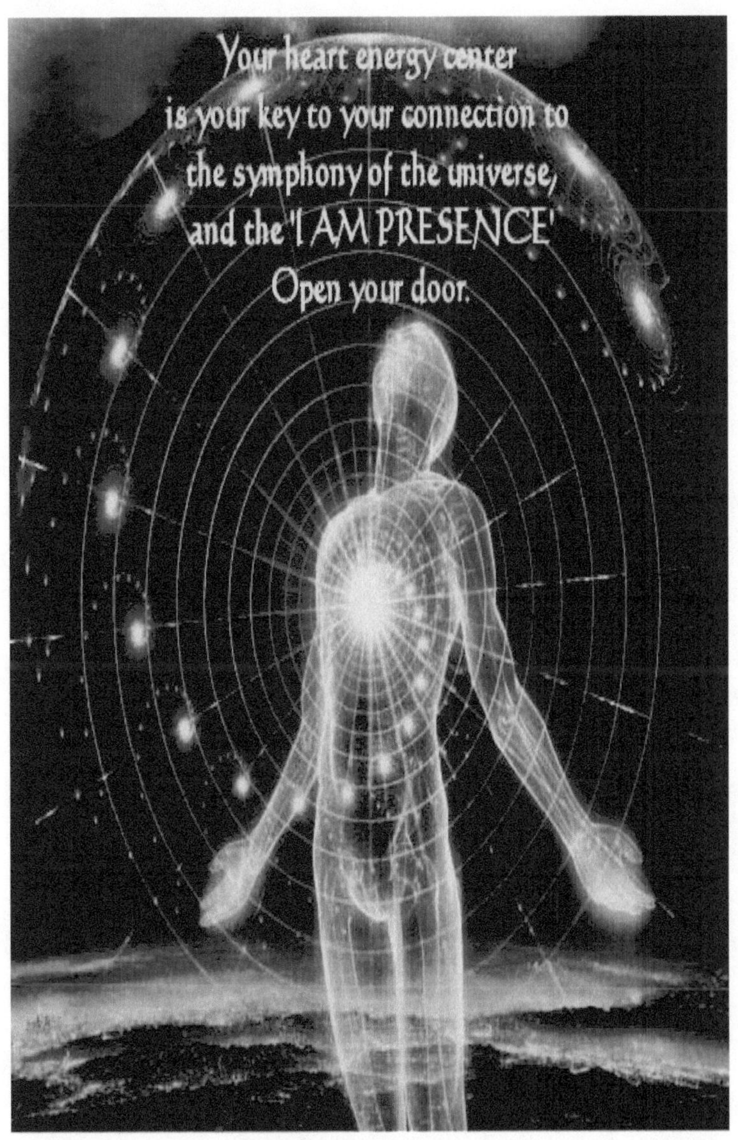

CHAPTER SIX

The Scientific Process Of Cellular Transmutation Of The Natural Biological Star Gate Passage Of Ascension Via Celestalline Light Waves

Celestalline stardust blue, white powder gold is a natural transient (very short life) element. The ancient Egyptians tried to find them in the substance called white gold powder, and also tried to manufacture it.

The substance only appears during the process of natural biological Star Gate passage Ascension when the body transmutes temporarily into light and rides in the Celesteline wave and then it remanifests outside Time and Space in the Eternal Spirit realms.

When the process of natural biological
Star Gate passage happens, the body
leaves a (pale blue) powder residue.
Celesteline that many have tried to
eagerly collect in ancient times in
Egypt, and they also tried to chemically
create it as a white or gold powder.
By the way white powder gold and
other types of monoatomic substance
that some are using these days, that are
on the market as supplements, they are
promoted to advance and accelerate
the process of Molecular Compaction.
What this does when ingested is it
radically stimulates the introduction of
higher Dimensional currents, but out
of order and if your Templates are
damaged, without the Twelve
Dimension Sub-Harmonic carrier
wave, you get a rush and feel better for
a while, but your Templates are
eroding right underneath you. It also
creates a dependency of the body and
in the long run your body gets sicker
faster.
You don't need to take artificial white

powder gold, it is a trickery, since you have the ability to use your mind to run your body in a way that before long you will be able to manufacture your own Celesteline form inside out. Celesteline is actually created in the DNA, it comes out in the Hydrogen bonds that link together the DNA helix spirals and those hydrogen molecules change in the process of cellular transmutation, this the place where the element Celesteline forms, that only activates for the purpose of bodily transmutation as part of the natural chemical process of metamorphosis, when we transcend the Holographical DNA Biotechnology Light Time Matrix, to outside time and space in the Eternal realms of Spirit. Upon contact with oxygen, liquid Celestalline secretions dry to a fine powder which rapidly breaks down into inert elemental units. Celestalline powder is a natural biochemical by product secreted by the body during Star Gate passage, or upon death of the physical avatar if the residing Consciousness is able to achieve Star Gate ascension out of Density. Pure Celestalline powder can be collected in minute amounts gently dusting the skin after one has passed through a Star Gate and remanifests outside Time and Space on the other side in the Eternal Spirit realms. If it is rapidly collected and specifically stored, pure Celestalline powder is a powerful healing agent because it can trigger temporary burst of the Twelve Strand DNA Template activation for anchoring an individual's Twelveth Dimensional Divine Schematic Blueprint.

Long ago in the times of ancient Egypt impure Celestalline powder or its old aged residue would be harvested from the corpses of mummies whenever they were discovered. Impure Celestalline powder is known as White Powder Gold or White Powder Celestalline that was used by the

Anunnaki Illuminati Pharaohs to trigger psychic powers by way of unnatural activation of the Eleven higher strands of there DNA template, this process led to permanent disability of the lower DNA strands, that lead to physical addiction to the substance and eventually insanity.

I think this interesting topic point is important to discuss, that our bodies from birth never get back certain elements that we are born with that are known as Star Dust, this Star Dust allows us to operate these biological animated avatars at there absolute optimal levels, allowing us to run our electrical curcuits and electromagnetic fields at a clearer and faster rate, this then allows us with these eight natural colloidal metals to no longer operate on a Copper Wiring system anymore and to start operating on a Fibre Optic wiring system that enables us to process a Thousand times more information in every second. So we can

completely upgrade our avatars by way of diet and with spiritual disciplines and practices, and by the conscious manifesting of these elements, by raising the bodies vibration, we are then creating these elements within our own Luminous Energy information software field. But some people do ingest these eight colloidal metallic metals in there purest forms to try to kick start this process. The Star Dust elements are eight colloidal metals (gold, silver, platinum, palladium, ruthenium, rhodium, osmium, iridium), and once the Oraphim human biological avatar has the eight colloidal elements flowing in its system, after they are able to access their dormant Ten stands of DNA, and by activating them we can access are our Eternal Oraphim Angelic Human Light Bodies. We then can open a Sixty foot field of Light around our Luminous Energy fields and travel through the Planets atmospheres, through the Porthole filiments of the

Suns from Solar System to Solar System then travelling from Galaxy to Galaxy. The eight colloidal metals create a metallic ceramic field around the body, so that it cannot burn up as we travel throught the extremely heated temperatures of the Planets atmospheres. No Space Crafts Needed, for we are the Eternal Divine Intrinsic Transcendental Energetic Consciousness of Spirit. Monatominc elements are a super conductor at room temperature and they show charcteristics of energy production and so can receive, save, and release Light information energy with out any loss, its the electrons bond with the anti electrons from opposite momentum Light bands that rotate around the oval nucleus. These monatomic elements like gold simultaneously then creates a Light Prana Vortex that is spiralling along a double helix through the atom nucleus, that equates to Kundalini Energy. It also creates an independent Zero Magnetic field around itself, which equates to the Merkaba energy field of the Light Body. The Merkaba is the Light Body of ascended human beings, which actually means Mer - light bands bonded together and rotating in opposite directions, Ka - energy of Life and Spirit, Ba - Soul, so Mer-Ka-Ba = Spiritual power of Life, so the Soul melt together and form a unity that creates Light bands that rotate in opposite directions that surmount Space and Time, Mer-Ka-Ba also translates to Human Light Body. So the element monatonic gold also does not lose energy or function and its durability is ever lasting, so pure monatomic gold also levitates under certain conditions interacting with the Planets electromagnetic field. When created naturally in the human avatar or ingested and interacted with on a Consciously Spiritual level a connection in union is formed as One, it is then absorbed into the body, it then enhances the energetic conductivity of DNA up to Ten thousand times, then the aging process is reversed by the energetic repair of defective DNA programs, it appears to be full of strength like a fresh cell that is vibrant and then expands the vital DNA Life span. All cells are repaired and regenerated to there fullest capacity to operate, the endocrine gland system is energetically activated to full strength including the Pineal, Thymus and Pituitary gland, and our self healing powers activate, as the flow of Light Quantum photons within the Nerve system and Meridian system is increased and then intensifies permantently on a continuum, and is then in alignment with the Zero Point energy field of the Creation's Matrix, then able to manifest at a rapid pace and interact and Transverse the Energy fields of the Matrix inside Time and Space in this Holographical DNA Biotechnology Creation and outside Time and Space in the Eternal Spirit realms.

The Oraphim Angelic Human Eternal Light Body Activation

The Connection To Monatomic Elements Of Star Dust

The connection between gold and biological life well not just gold, but all the orbitally rearranging monatomic elements is symbiotic to the nature of the design of this super advanced DNA biotechnology.

If we look at the elements that we are made up of when we are born into this world, we never get those elements back into our bodies again from food or water these are Gold, Silver, platinum, Palladium, Ruthenium, Rhodium, Osmium, Iridium, these trace mineral elements that we need in our DNA to function correctly at our ultimate potential and then allow us to evolve. So you can ingest and take Ormus a chemical potion an extract of colloidal ocean minerals that empowers and uplifts, with doses of 50ml a day for expansion and clarity, in this potions make up there is a mineral content of 70% monotonic gold and 30% magnesium for long life and good health. Rhodium if you cap the DNA molecule of Rhodium it becomes a lot more electrically charged or conductive, also zeolite removes toxic metals from the body through urine discharge and its intelligent, so it takes out uranium first then mercury and so on down the poisonous metal chart, the above most toxic metals to the human biological system are then removed from body. So by taking these trace elements and removing radicals from the body, this then helps with alining the DNA for its works – it then functions correctly with the right voltage, if the DNA is not at the right voltage, we can't heal ourselves and if DNA is not at the right voltage we cannot evolve beyond were we are at in evolution at the present moment, once the DNA is at the right voltage we can evolve to homo-luminous to access our light bodies, to stop the cycles of life and death and open portholes above and outside of our bodies through the Chakra system to access the Hyper-Dimensional Matrix.

The Hyper-Dimensional Matrix is made up of rainbow spectrums of Light, with resonance, vibration that creates sacred geometry patterns times five to create this Three Dimensional reality and the other higher Dimensional realities in the living Hollogram of Light for us to transverse, to travel in via wormholes, portholes that are filaments connected from Sun to Sun, Solar System to Solar System, Galaxy to Galaxy. So we need these fundamental elements to function at the biological and Spiritual levels to access our true potential, of our true nature. Ormus means orbitally rearrange monotonic elements, these are called micro clusters, meaning if you allow atoms to come out of a syringe nozzle each atom one at a time, they will cluster into geometric sacred geometry patterns, three dimensional, like a cube, octahedron, dodecahedron, icosahedron and the molecules form into these three dimensional geometric patterns and when it has this structure, it is more electrically charged, more resistance on the outside of the geometric structure, much harder and more resilient and has more resistance to temperature, to wear and tear, it has all these amazing qualities and nourishes the body.

The sacred geometry structures are so important because its living and we are made up of geometric matter, they are the smallest particles, beyond the electrons that we are made up of, and in the future when we can open our Light Bodies ascending to the highest levels of the Universe, that will allow us to transverse the multiverses travelling multidimensionally, in the Universes of the Cosmic Matrix of Light, of Life, because all geometry is alive every cell, every particle of the Universe, is alive.

The true science of the Universe is sacred geometry created by vibration, resonance of Light, and each note, key of resonance is related to different spectrums of Light from the full rainbow spectrum, originating from the Source Field that emmited the Three Primal Sound Fields of the Blue Light Consciousness Field, the Gold Light Consciousness Field and the Violet Light Consciousness Field.

So by changing electromagnetic flux fields, we can open up portholes, we can open up the porthole above our bodies by opening and accessing our Crown Chakra and with our Luminous Energy field around our body's, a foot above our heads, a foot below our feet and as wide as our arms stretch outwards we can expand our Luminous Energy fields to a sixty foot wide field of Light and travel transversing the Universe in our body's of Light through the Hyper-Dimensional portholes, Light filaments, by changing the electromagnetic flux fields, we can heal our body's accessing different energy fields in DNA.

Monatomic elements are simply elements that are stable as single atoms (Mona refers to Mono meaning something being ONE). The monatomic elements are installing (Gold tipped wires on your brain synapse), so in other words the monatomic elements are transforming our wiring from copper wiring to being wired with Fibre Optics, where the same width of wiring is able to carry One thousand times as much processing of information.

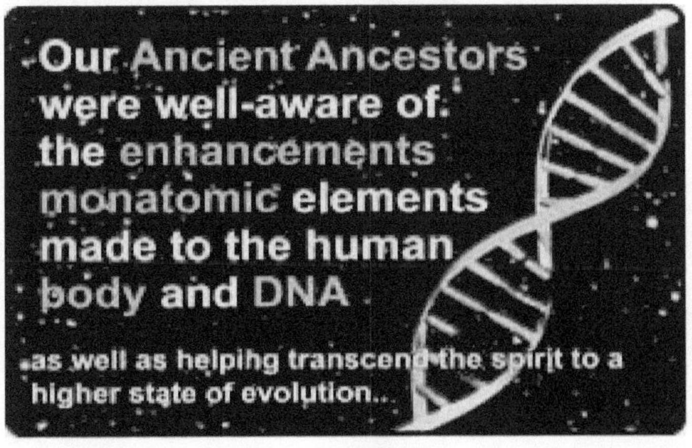

Image is of an Atomic Symbol with a
Yellow Light Flare.

Image is an abstract concept of Atom and
Quantum Waves illustrated with Fractal
Elements.

CHAPTER SEVEN

Manifesting Control Of The Mind By Creating A Bridge Between the Subconscious & Conscious mind

By Way Of

Consciousness Meaning Eternal Spirit & Matter The Three Dimensional Sacred Geometric Structure Of DNA

So how do we define the mechanism with which the human mind exercises the function of consciousness, and how do we describe the way in which the consciousness operates to deduce meaning from the causing and responding to the stimulus it receives, so lets consider the fundamental character of the material information that it receives from the Worlds enveloping environment from our physical existence. So matter and energy tend to be misleading because there are two different states of existence in the physical World that we are living in, one being matter the other being energy, now matter is said to be a solid substance as opposed to energy which is understood to mean a force of some sort, this is misleading, because science now knows that both the electrons that spin in the energy field located around the nucleus of the atom and the nucleus itself are made up of oscilating energy grids. So solid matter in the strict construction of the term simply does not exist, because the atomic structure is composed of oscilating energy grids that's surrounded by other oscilating energy grids, which operate at extrodinary high speeds. So the energy grid that composes the nucleus of the atom, and vibrates at approximately ten to the power of twenty two Herz, which means ten followed by twenty two zeros and also at seventy degrees farenheight, so the atom osilates at the power of ten to the power of five Herz. So an entire molecule that's composed of an entire number of atoms is bound together in a single energy field and vibrates in the range of ten Herz, so a living cell vibrates at approximately one hundred and three Herz, the point is that the entire human biological avatar, its brain and Consciousness combined is a set of very complex systems of energy fields, and the same is said for the entire Hyper-Dimensional Matrix of realities. These energy fields are the so called states of matter and are different variations of states of energy. So Consciousness is a function of the interaction of energy in two opposite states, which are motion verses stillness or rest. So energy creates, stores and retrieves energy in the Universe by projecting and expanding at certain frequencies, so we can perceive in a three dimensional model that then creates a living pattern that's known as a hologram, the perception and conception of the hologram is understood, by imagining a pond of water and dropping several stones into the water and as the ripples are created by the three stones simultaneously and are raditating outwards to the edge of the pond, then if you imagine the pond is instantly frozen, so that the ripple patterns are preserved instantly, then if the ice is removed leaving the three stones in the bottom of the pond, and then the ice is exposed to a powerful coherent source of light like say a lazer the result of this will be a three dimensional model, and so then can be perceived as a representation of the three stones suspended in mid air, like a hologram. Holograms are capable of encoding lots of detail that you can perceive like this. Also it is possible to take a holographical projection of bog water and view it through magnification and you will then see tiny organisms that are not visible by the eye. Another way of perceiving a hologram is that if you have a pattern and split it in parts, it will be distorted a little, but a projection of the pattern would be made and replicated and reformed entirely to the whole pattern image in holographical form.

The fundamentals to creating a hologram is that energy in motion must interact with energy in a state of rest, so if we go back to the pond and stones analogy, the stones represent energy in motion, the water represents energy in a state of rest, so to activate or in effect to perceive the meaning of a holograph, energy must be passed through the interference pattern that's generated by interactions between the moving energy, and then the energy at rest. Then with coherent light focused on the frozen interference pattern you can produce a three dimensional holographical image into a space. Another characteristic of the hologram is its efficient consistency, as billions maybe even trillions of pieces of information can be stored in a single tiny space. So a thread of massive, gigantic preportions of information on a continuum in a multi-layered and multidimensional pattern, that can be stored in a single minute space of the Creation and replicate its self in its entirity. This is why if we take one cell of the Universe a human cell or a leave cell any cell you can recreate the entire Universe with all it bountiful variations of life in its entrity. So the Universe is compromised of interacting energy fields some in motion and some in a state of rest, building and creating the Sacred Geometric structure of this complex holographical Universe and beyond the Hyper-Dimensional Holographical Matrix.

So as energy passes through various aspects of the Hyper-Dimensional hologram and is perceived by the electrostatic fields which comprise the human mind, the holographical images that are being conveyed are projected upon those electrostatic fields of the mind and are perceived or understood to the extent that the electrostatic field is operating at a frequency in amplitude that can harmonise with, and therefore read the energy carrier wave pattern passing through it, then changes in the frequency and amplitude of the electrostatic field which comprises the mind and determines the configuration, and so creates the charcter of the holographic energetic matrix which the mind then projects, by intercept meaning directly from the holographic transmissions of the Universe and Hyper-Dimensional Matrix.

So for the Mind to make sense of what the holographical images are saying to it, the Mind proceeds to compare the image just received with its Self specifically, mirroring, it does this by comparing the image received with that part of its own hologram which constitutes as memory, so by registering differences in different geometric forms, and an energy frequency that Consciousness perceives. So then perceiving the realization that the Mind does not create Consciousness but instead Eternal Divine Spirit that is Source Ultra Violet energetic Consciousness, creates the physical biological animated Avatar and builds the brain all within the Luminous Energy Field, that is the Software that informs the Hardware the DNA of super advanced Biotechnology to grow the physical biological Avatar, and it is Spirit Consciousness that has created the illusion of Mind.

We need to have focused and inhanced strength and attention to gain intuitive knowledge and Universal access leading to Universal Cosmic wisdom, and this then allows amplitude and frequency of brain wave output between the two sides of the brain, so

that it alters our Consciousness states to a higher elevation, this moves our Consciousness outside the physical dimensional sphere, so to ultimately escape any restrictions of time and space, this allows access to the higher intuitive levels of knowledge and wisdom that the Universe offers. Then one can then connect and travel in the holographical Universes Conciousness Matrix of multidimensional realities.
So we need to connect the human Luminous Energy field with the electromagnetic field of the heart and brain as one Unifed field to interact with the Earths electromagnetic field at a higher frequency and with an amplified electromagnetic field of the heart this allows us to manifest rapidly the surrounding enveloping reality in which to experience living life.
So we need to build a bridge from the Unconscious Mind to the Conscious Mind with light filaments through frequency and meditation, so we need to Unite the left side of the brain with

the right side of the brain to gain higher levels of Consciousness and experiences on multidimensional levels. When the left and right hemispheres of the brain are synchronized you can then receive higher levels of Consciousness and gain access to Universal and Cosmic Consciousness and can travel in these other dimensions.

This can be achieved with binaural beats at very low frequencies because they cause the right and left hemispheres of the brain to become unifed and synchronized these are the states and frequencies and effects.

Theta state 4-8Hz produces creativity, insight, dreams, deep meditation, and reduced Consciousness.

Gamma state 32-100Hz produces heightened perception, learning, and problem solving.

Beta state 13-32Hz produces awake,

alert Consciousness, thinking, and excitement.

Alpha state 8-13Hz produces a relaxed feeling both physically and mentally.

Delta state 0.5-4Hz produces repair, deep dreamless sleep, cellular repair, loss of bodily awareness and can cause an out of body experience.

So the right hemisphere is where you get your creativity, imagination, and emotions, your left hemisphere is very analytical and logical, it operates in a more binary method such as, yes or no or on and off, similar to how a computer works, so when you sync both sides of the brain you pretty much put your left side to sleep while keeping the right side of the brain active, this state allows the Mind to bypass the screening process that your left brain usually does. So hypnosis accesses the Subconscious Mind and permits direct access to the Subconscious Mind, which is in the right hemisphere and disengages the left hemisphere, when this harmony is achieved it opens doorways to portholes to allow you to go beyond yourself and tap into your full Chi Life Force Power. You then can access higher dimensions and also your past, present, and future experiences. Its your brain waves that effect the uniting of the left and right brain hemispheres, and when you have calm thoughts you can access your alpha state and then even more deeply in the theta state and deeper still in the delta state, and this state is usually only achieved by high functioning meditators like Buddhist Monks, Tribal peoples, Vegetalistas, Curanderos, and Shamans.

So as we know everything vibrates at frequency and when listening to binaural beats one frequency is heard in one ear and another frequency is heard in the other ear. Your brain then harmonizes these frequencies to create a lower brain wave than your normal frequency, this helps you achieve theta and delta states much faster. And it is known that 4-7Hz is the ideal frequency to produce having an out of body experience.

So when the Mind is in expanded states of Consciousness the right hemisphere of the brain is non linear its holistic and has a non verbal mode of functioning and acts as the primary matrix receptor for the holographical input, and when operating in phase or in coherence with the right side of the brain and then the left side of the brain provides the secondary matrix through its binary code and method of functioning to process the information data by comparison and then reduces it to distinct various two dimensional geometric shaped forms.

So when the brain is cohesively Unifed the left and right sides of the brain are functioning as One, then the directed manifesting energy through the Hearts electromagnetic field into the Planets electromagnetic field, and into the

Creations electromagnetic field, is amplified to create physical Geometric Matter into form creating realities in those fields at a much faster and rapid pace of manifesting.

Now meditation has similar uses to hypnosis and bineral beats but it is an entirely different technique to using frequency to harmonize both sides of the brain. Meditation is intense and protracted with a single minded concentration on the process of drawing energy up the spine activating your Kundalini Energy Life Force up into the Pineal Gland to access your Third Eye and attain multidimensional Consciousness and access to the Creation. This process ultimately results in the Creation of acoustic standing waves in the cerebral cortex on the right side of the brain.

We now know everything and everyone is connected in our entire Universe on the subatomic level, so what we think of as solid matter is actually energy in vibrations, everything is energy and all connected as One, in a Unifed Zero Point Energy field, the Quantum field. We know our emotions are energy so all that we feel and think is influencing everyone and everything, so that means our Minds are immaterial and held in the Quantum field. We now also know the Universe is an entanglement of energy waves at different densities and that we perceive them as matter particles that are in fact stimulated excited excitations of the Quantum field. So the heart and brain are connected through the dura which is the cushion between your spinal fluid and the brain, when the brain and heart are vibrating at the same frequency the heart then produces an electromagnetic energy field that is so powerful that it is five thousand times more powerful than the normal electromagnetic field it normally produces, this then amplifying your manifesting power into the Creation. And also when the brain and heart are on the same frequency, it is that powerful that it covers the circumference of forty thousand kilometres, that's the distance of the circumference of the Planet Gaia our Mother Earth known as Pachamana. This frequency band is so powerful it can break through metal, concrete, water, all and any structure, so when you raise your vibrational frequency you are influencing the planets magnetic charge of the entire Planet.

Studies of quantum entanglement have showed and proved and established the existence of nonlocal Consciousness, by taking two related particles and separated them into two different locations, they spun one particle and instantly the other twin partical started to spin in the other seperate location, so they were communicating to one another, the two particles were in an entangled quantum state.

When the body is in state of cohesive alignment it turns into a cohesive osilator and then vibrating in harmony with the surrounding eletro static medium, to achieve this one must build up the electromagnetic field around the body, this then allows you to access energy from the Earths electromagnetic field, this puts the body in harmony with the surrounding energy fields in the environment, allowing movement of the seat of Consciousness into the enveloping environment. This is because the two electromagnetic mediums the fields are United as a continuum field, so on a singular energetic continuum, so the same process moves the brain into focus coherence and into higher levels of frequency and amplitude. So to train in algorithms of frequencies allowing Universal data collection and then promotes the bodies energy levels, to the point the person can adequately experience out of body movement. So with this the body is resonating with the Planet's electromagnetic sphere, the human body then creates a powerful carrier wave, this assits the Mind in communication with other minds that are also in tune to these frequencies. So this allows a completely new way of experiencing your encompassing reality, with Conscious perception changed into a Conscious understanding of the oscilating energy grid systems, and muli-layered dimensions that we all reside within.

When the alignment of the two hemispheres of the brain are United and Connected they are now on a single energy Continuum, so when the brain is in a Unifed relationship it is in this coherence state.

So the Mind is a hologram which attunes its self to the Universal hologram by the medium of energy exchanged, and so there by deducing meaning and then achieving the state of Conscious Awareness which we call Consciousness. Consciousness is a Divine Ultra Violet energy also known as Spirit that fluctuates outside time and space and inside time and space, in these super advanced DNA technological structured Hyper-Dimensional holograms, and Spirit is able to fold in and out of all possiblitties of the Creation, the Brahman, the Whole.

So with Ancient practices, Spiritual ceremonies, and diet of which is key and with frequencies we can then change our conditions to get a refinement in the energy matrix of the Mind by expanding and changing Human Consciousness altering it to a higher optimal plane of functioning, then we can by pass operating on just the physical senses, then the Hyper-Dimensional holographical Matrix can be deciphered, and understood and absolutely completely comprehended in its entirety. As one Ancient advanced holographical living biological technology of the Sacred Geometric structures of the Scaffolding of Life know as DNA, created inside time and space dimensions of reality, and that is operated by Spirit, Divine Ultra Violet energetic Consciousness from the Kingdoms of Light in the Eternal realms outside time and space.

So how do we understand and perceive the Cosciousness process well if we visualize the holographical input with a three dimensional grid system then super imposed over it, were all the energy patterns are contained within, so then we can describe it in terms of three dimensional geometry using mathematics to reduce the information data to a two dimensional geometric form. So then the Mind is operating like any digital computer system that works on the level of binary code. So when the Mind composes a three dimensional matrix over holographical information it wishes to interpret and then reduces that information automatically to a two dimensional Sacred Geometric form, it can totally process it by using its fundamental binary code system, and process gigantic amounts of information data and then makes various comparisons between the data and information that is stored in its memory, this is just how the Mind works, functions and operates. The Mind perceives by comparison only by the past and present environments and experiences it has related to in past memory, that is stored in the crystal memory banks. So we realize that our surrounding and encompassing realities are built and constructed on this constant fluctuating comparisons of what we are perceiving, whether that's feelings from the heart, our brainwaves, or our vocalized words and from all the senses of the Sacred Geometric biological Avatar body. So we only perceive the differences always on a continuum, with different states of expanded Consciousness.

I think it is important to immerse ourselves in these subjects and perceive the understanding with clarity of Eternal Consciousness, and that of ancient knowledge and wisdom to operate at our fullest potential, I find all of the above discussed energies and forces of life that are natures essence, that of Spirit and of the forces behind the building blocks of Sacred Geometry that constructs the Scaffolding of Life into animated living experience, its just intrinsically magicial.

A MOLECULES OSILATING ENERGY FIELDS

CHAPTER EIGHT

Science of the Super Advanced Biological Technology of DNA & the Blueprint Design of the Angelic Human Avatar

So after researching all the ancient texts and information on a varity of subjects we can conclude that the Universe, the Hyper-Dimensional Matrix of Cosmoses, of matter, of DNA is the most powerful advanced technology in this Universe and beyond, allowing us Eternal Spirits of the spectrum of Ultra Violet Divine energetic light Source Consciousness, to manifest into these Cosmoses of Multiverses from the Kingdoms of Light in the Eternal realms outside time and space. We Eternal Spirits come through white wormholes then exiting out of black wormholes into a particular Universe, then we manifest from within our Luminous Energy Fields the Avatar of the race of species, in which we have chosen to have an experience of being, living as that race to get a different perspective of perceiving the Universe and the whole Creation from that races perceived Mindsets, and to grow Spiritually, and for some Souls to wake up Consciously to realize that they have a mission while manifesting in that race of species, to help in there evolution, to raise Consciousness, to teach ancient texts of wisdom and knowledge of Spiritual practices, of healing, and many other reasons like helping in Wars of dark and light, fighting negative agendas of Self Service races of many species.

So within our Luminous Energy field which is the Software that informs the Hardware the DNA to grow the biological Avatar by building the cells with the building blocks of life, that's the Sacred Geometry of the dodecahedrons and the corners of the dodecahedrons are the only solid of the structure and the corners are fed by the amino acids from the food we ingest, and inside the dodecahedrons are the tetrahedrons and the corners of this structure are the only solids of its form and the cornrers are fed by the proteins in the food we ingest. Now the tetrahedron spins inside the dodecahedrons in up to a hundred and twenty patterns, the different patterns are to create different forms of DNA to manifest and form different species, to experience.

Another awesome part of the Universes design is how tower blocks of dodecahedron crystals form that then in turn naturally by design attract molecules of DNA to then wind and wrap around the crystal tower blocks of dodecahedrons in at least a double spiral to form DNA helix strands, as related to genomics a term which is used to describe the physical structure of DNA, the DNA molecule is made of the two linked strands entwinded, each strand has a backbone made of alternating sugar deoxyribose and phosphate groups, and connected in the centre by hydrogen bonding, the hydrogen bonds form between nucleotides, the repeating unit of DNA and the language of the genetic code.

The truth is we human beings have twelve strands of DNA but only have two strands active, this is by design from our enslaving farmer race Creators, which in all ancient texts, artifacts, sculpures, and oral traditions Worldwide state that our genetic manipulator Creators are the Draco Reptilian race and their half breeds of human and reptilian shape shifters known as the Anunnaki, that use this Planet of humans as slaves for their service of many things like building infrastructure, because we humans are amazing iniative creators of construction, engineering and problem solving, we also are ambidextrous the ability to use either of our nible hands to skilfully preform a infinite variety of tasks, they also like to use humans to fight there Wars and for blood consumption, sacrifice and for harvesting Loosh energy.

So when humanity was genetically manipulated, our twelve strands of DNA genetics were reverse engineered and degraded by the negative Anunnaki. So humanity were only given access to two strands of DNA and most of humans DNA is typically packaged into forty six chromosomes located in the cells nucleus, which is a specialized compartment for storing DNA, each chromosome in the nucleus is made up of two linear DNA strands wrapped interwined around each other over a tower block of dodecahedrons. The human cells also contain a small amount of extra chromosomal DNA located in another part of the cell called the mitochondria, this mitochondrial DNA is a lot more like bacterial DNA, a single long circular piece of DNA made up of two strands of DNA. A DNA strand is a long thin molecule with a width of two billionths of a meter or known as two nanometers and put into size perspective that's about forty thousand times smaller than a human hair, by being this thin this means they can be compacted tightly so they can fit correctly into the ratio of a cell. The length of a DNA strand if it were laid out and stretched in one line would be six point six feet or just over two meters, so much information storage, so if we used a tennis ball as an example of the size of the nucleus of a cell it would have the equivalent amount of DNA compacted inside of about eight miles long, an absolute information highway of data storage.

All DNA strands share a common structure composed of the building blocks known as nucleotides that are connected together in a row, they are compromised of three joined parts, a sugar molecule, a phosphate group and a nitrogenous base. So these sugars of one nucleotide connect to the phosphates of the adjacent nucleotide to create and form the exterior of the DNA strand, these are known as the sugar phosphate backbone, then the interior of the DNA strand is created from the nitrogenous bases, then these bases bind together in pairs that form faint bonds that hold the two strands of DNA together in the serpent double hexi structure, and so their sequence encodes the organisms genetic information. The two DNA strands are connected together by pairing between the nitrogenous bases in the nucleotides of each strand, the nitrogenous base of a DNA nucleotide can be one of four different molecules which are, (A) adenine, (G) guanine, (T) thymine and (C) cryosine. So these pairs of nitrogenous bases on opposing strands are bonded together by attractions that are called hydrogen bonds that wll occur in a specific pattern. So every adenine on one DNA strand will form two hydrogen bonds with a thymine molecule on the complementary strand and vice versa, and every guanine molecule on one strand forms three hydrogen bonds with a cytosine molecule on the other and vice versa, so in this formatted way the two strands of DNA are bonded together by hydrogen bonds all along their entire length, this then creates the forming of the steps of the spiral staircase that is the double serpent the double helix. The two strands of DNA are antiparallel to each other this means that the two strands run parallel to one another but they operate and run in opposite directions, this is for energy flows of a circuitry. So this means that where the backbone of one DNA strand starts with a sugar molecule and finishes in a phosphate group, the backbone of its complementary strand starts with a phosphate group and finishes in a sugar molecule, so the antiparallel orientation of the two DNA strands builds DNA more structurally stable and enables the complementary base pairing that holds and connects the DNA strands together. So the direction of each DNA strand is significant to the process of copying the DNA by replication and able to read the information contained in the genes of DNA the transcription, because the cells can only read DNA in one direction, because the cells only read DNA by starting with the sugar end of the backbone and ending with a phosphate end, the building blocks of cells and the energies and forces behind all life are just majestic, just pure magical in nature and Spirit energies.

So if this human seven point zero version of humanity we are manifesting as now in the present day on this Planet Earth had access to its twelve completed all firing strands of DNA, we would be considered one of the most advanced species in the Universe and Creation, for we could access the Zero Point Energy Fields of Creation, be psychic, we could use telekinesis, open up a sixty foot wide field of light around our avatar body's and travel through atmospheres of Planets and then travel through the Sun portholes Solar System to Solar System and Galaxy the Galaxy, this will happen when you can connect your Chakras with the Planet Chakra, the Solar System Chakra, the Galaxy Chakra and the Universal Chakra Systems. We could also teleport munltidimensionally anywhere in the Universe, and when your Heart Chakra that floats in front of your main Heart Chakra is activated you can connect and travel Universe to Universe, travelling in the whole Cosmos of Multiverses. By design our twelve stranded genetics once fully activated have the power to repair any distorted fractual damage to the electromagnetic field of the Planet, and the electromagnetic fields of the Galaxy and the Universe.

After all we are truly Eternal Immortal Interdimensional Light beings of Ultra Violet Divine energetic Consciousness also known as Spirit.

Did you know that your souls DNA is called your source code and there is a long number to it, and that this is your souls registration and that the first temple always has been and always will be you, your physical human avatar vessel temple. Known as the temple of man or tabernacle of man, in texts of the bible the tabernacle is actually an extract blueprint of the human body and it correlates all the functions of the body, that is also called the tabernacle of witness, we are supposed to be a witness or a dwelling place of the kingdom, we should be the kingdom, the kings domain. But until we can transmit our frequency energies through the veil of A.I fields and other suppressing technologies and connect our Meridian Energy Systems to our Chakra Systems accessing our Pineal Gland in the centre of the brain and activate our dormant ten strands of DNA, we are blocked from the Zero Point Energy Field and so we are blocked from a true connection to Spirit, God or Source which is known in Universal terms as Manna.

Then when you begin contemplating on connecting the dots of Conscious Spirit Energy, that resides in the Eternal realms outside time and space and its interaction with this holographical Hyper-Dimensional Matrix of multi Cosmoses of living biological life, then you can perceive the four fundamental energies that allow it to exist and operate and function, which are the strong and weak nuclear forces, electromagnetism and gravity, these combined energies allow us to manifest into the holographical Creation, which allows the Souls Ultra Violet Divine

Source Energetic Consciousness to be able to stay and operate within these living biological dimensions of light frequency spectrums. Then you can perceive down to the atoms and cell structures that are built from Sacred Geometry, then down to the nucleus, protons and electrons, it is fascinating and we all should know intrically how to operate this super advanced biological living Human Avatar with our Spirit Consciousness and understand that we are Gods and Goddesses, that are the Creators of our enveloping realities.

So in solids electrons are the primary means of conducting current because protons are larger and typically bound to a nucleus and so more difficult to move, but in liquids current carriers are more often ions.
So an electron is a stable negatively charged component of an atom, also electrons exist outside of surrounding the atom nucleus, so each electron

carries one unit of negative charge $(1.602 \times 10^{-19}$ this is the basic unit of electric charge equal to the quantity of charge transferred in one second, by a steady current of one ampere) and has a small mass as compared with that of a neutron or photon, electrons are much less massive than neutrons or protons, the mass of an electron is $(9.10938 \times 10^{-31 \text{ kg}})$, this is about the mass of a proton.

In quantum mechanics electrons are considered to be identical to each other because no intrinsic physical property may be used to distinguish between them, electrons may swap positions with each other without causing an observable change in a system. Electrons are considered to be a type of elementary particle because they are not made up of smaller components, they are a type of particle belonging to the lepton family and have the smallest mass of any charged lepton or any other charged particle. So electrons are attracted to positive charged particles such as protons, regardless or not if a substance has a net charge, as this is determined by the balance between the number of electrons and also the positive charge of atomic nuclei, so if there are more electrons than positive charges a material is is then said to be negatively charged, so if the number of electrons and protons are balanced a material is then said to be electrically neutral. Electrons can also exist free in a vacuum these are called free electrons and electrons in the substances of metals behave as if they were free electrons and can move to produce a net flow of charge named an electric current, so when electrons or even photons move a magnetic field is generated. So a neutral atom has the same number of photons and electrons, it also can have a variable number of neutrons these form isotopes since neutrons do not carry a net electrical charge. These electrons have properties of both particles and waves, they can be diffracted like photons but yet they can collide with each other and other particles like other matter particles. When you look at the atomic theory it describes electrons as surrounding the proton-neutron nucleus of an atom in shells, so while its possible for an electron to be found any where in an atom it is very probable to find one in its shell, also an electron has a spin or intrinsic angular momentum of (1/2). Its been found that the largest electron in radius is (10^{-22}) meters, electrons are point charges that are electrical charges with no physical dimensions, fascinating that they have no physical dimensions.

So when this Universe was created by the three primal sound waves after the initial explosive force was emmited, it then waned and decreased in size, gradually in strength, intensity and size, the number of surviving protons, electrons and neutrons began to interact with one another and they formed atoms, and so these chemical bonds are a result of transfers and or sharing of electrons between atoms.

So a protons stable subatomic particle that has a positive charge equal in magnitude to a unit of electron charge and a mass of (1.67262 x 10^{-27} kg) which is (1.836) times the mass of an electron.
The structural understanding of the nature of the proton within the group of subatomic particles is that protons and neutrons have been shown to be made up of smaller particles and are classified as baryons these particles are comprosed of three elementary units of matter known as quarks.
A proton is a positively charged particle that resides within the atomic nucleus, so the number of protons in the atomic nucleus is what determins the atomic number of an element, as shown in the elements on the periodic table, so in the standard of quantum physics in the quark model it is known that the proton is compromised of one

down quark two up quarks which is mediated by gluons in the quantum model. So the proton is in the atomic nucleus it is a nucleon and has a spin of (-1/2) it is known as a fermion, and is comprosed of three quarks meaning it is a triquark baryon a type of hadron. The mass of a proton is ($938 \text{ MeV}/c^2 = 1.67 \times 10^{-27}$ kg) and the diameter of a proton is (1.65×10^{-15} m) and the charge of a proton is (+1 fundamental unit = 1.602×10^{-19} this is the basic unit of electric charge equal to the quantity of charge transferred in one second, by a steady current of one ampere). So protons together with electrically neutral particles called neutrons they make up all atomic nuclei except for the hydrogen nucleus which consists of a single proton, so all nucleus of a given chemical element has the same number of protons, this number defines the atomic number of an element and determines the position on the chart in the periodic table, so when the number of protons in a nucleus equals the number of electrons orbiting the nucleus, the atom is electrically neutral.

Protons that are from ionized hydrogen are given high velocities in particle accelerators and are commomly used as projectiles to produce and study nuclear reactions, so protons are the chief constituent of primary cosmic rays and are amidst the products of some types of artificial nuclear reactions.

So the nucleus is a specialized structure occurring in most cells but with the exception of blue and green alge bacteria and the cells are separated from the rest of the cell by a double layer which is the nuclear membrane, this membrane seems to be continuous with the endoplastic reticulum, a membranous network, of the cell and has pores, which allows permit of the entrance of large molecules, so the nucleus controls and regulates the activities of the cell, so its metabolism and its growth, and also carries the genes structures that contain the hereditary information from our past ancestors. The nucleoli are small bodies often seen within the nucleus, that is the gel looking matrix in which the nuclear componants are suspended that is the nucleoplasm. As we know the nucleus houses an organisms genetic code which determines the amino acid sequence of proteins critical for day to day function, as it primarily serves as the information centre of the cell, so this means the information in DNA is copied or transcribed into a range of messenger ribonucleic acid known as mRNA molecules, each of which encodes the information for one protein and in some cirumstances more than one protein which is bacteria. The mRNA molecules are then transported through the nuclear envelope into the cytoplasm this is where they are translated, these serving as templates for synthesis of specific proteins.

The reason I write about the electrons, protons, and nucleases is because we all need to understand the quantum mechanics of the cells of the Avatars we create and manifest via our Eternal Spirit Consciousness, and to then understand on the micron level of the Sacred Geometry building blocks of cells, and also then to understand the building elements of the Sacred Geometic structures, and the energetic forces that build and operate this super advanced Biotechnology of DNA, which are electromagnetism, gravity and the weak and strong nuclear forces that allow all physical life to exist, to become animated, lively, vigorous with activity, and so activated by Eternal Spirit Consciousness. Then we can operate our Avatars at our optimal performance and reconnect the dormant ten strands of DNA to reconnect all twelve strands of our DNA Consciously, to access our Diamond Sun Light Bodies and stop the cycles of life and death, so we can ascend, transcend into our Mer-Ka-Ba field, that is our birth rights as free Sovereign Eternal Light beings of the Creation. We are all Eternal Supreme beings with the permanent power of Authority of Self, no other beings have a right to rule over any Individual because we are all Angels of light, Goddesses and Gods, waking up to our true Eternal Identities, we are all equals on the level of Spirit, and equals in the Creation of DNA, by our Creative Conscious manifestions into the Fields of these Templar Light Time Matrix realities.

So after contemplating and trying to understand the forces of the nucleus and electrons and blackholes, the strong and weak nuclear forces that power the atom that of gravity Source energy, you can perceive what the strong force is, the strong force is what holds the protons together and what is the weak nuclear force, the weak nuclear force is what holds the electrons around the nucleus. There has been a mathematical contruct made that created a hypothesis, the hyperthetical theory called the strong force was created to explain how the photons and the nucleus and the atom hold together. Today a main stream scientist they would tell you there is four energy fields in the Universe that are electromagnetism, gravity and the strong nuclear force and the weak nuclear force.

The numbers with ten will be Sacred Geometry having a distinctive energetic boundry and the strong nucleus is exactly ten times more powerful than the weak nucleus, the ten times ratio between the strong nucleus and the weak nucleus is geometric, so if you dissolved particles completely and instead of particles in the nucleus, you have corners, solids an energy that is alive, living geometry in nature as in living geometric matter, with a living Spirit energy.

A basic for example is oxygen this has a cubical wave, it is a wave in a cubical shape wave as we know water does this naturally, there have been experiments with sand dropped in water and you can cause vibrations in the water and the sand forms shapes of geometric patterns. So long as you are creating even sounds in other words even sound waves like that of a singing bowel or on a key board player, the keys that are white that are dynatronic broadcast that you can hear or can be heard, so sound in the water creates form in the shape of geometry, geometric matter, shapes that are the wonderful World of Sacred Geometric Matter that are the building blocks of the Scaffolding of Life.

The behaviour of an atom and the behaviour of the blackhole are one and the same, a black hole is a gravity vortex, so what is an atom it is a gravity vortex and so the power behind the atom that powers it is gravity. So gravity what force is it, most do not understand that gravity is flowing in from a parrallel Universe (or really its flowing in from the dimension of the Eternal realm) where space and time do not exist. So gravity is flowing in through a blackhole that is the atomic nucleus and then flows back out again, is this how and why we are living multidimensionally all at the same time, is gravity Source energy, Spirit from the Eternal realm and this is what forms and creates the atom.

This explains wave particles and duality as its a wave and a particle, when it is a wave its behaviour is not local it does not have a specific location in space or in time. This is the Eternal realm outside of time and space, where we Spirits come from and are able to connect to all of the Whole, the Brahman, the Oneness of all that be, the Creation, the Hyper-Dimensional Matrix of advanced DNA holgraphical Biotechnology. This is why if we tap into our Consciousness we can transcend time and space and transverse the Universes in the whole Hyper-Dimensional Matrix and in the Eternal Spirit realms and move any where in the Creation. It is like a maze of a multi layered jigsaw that one can find solving at times you can feel perplexed, bemused even fazed, a puzzle of living matter, a mystery even an enigma and many paradoxes we have along the way of raising our Consciousness to solve this multi layered maze, that's in a many layered jigsaw puzzle of light energy vibrating, osilating into being on a continuum, Individually but also as One, One being of Consciousness energy fields, One sea of light energy.

So gravity is the Source of matter, gravity is the Eternal Spirit within us all and all around us in our manifested realities and in which ever species or race or Universe you are in and also outside time and space, in the Eternal realms, where we Eternal Interdimensional Light beings of Ultra Violet energetic Consciousness originate, from within the space that be. Remember there is more space than anything else in this Universe and the whole Hyper-Dimensional Matrix, including the cells of our Avatars. So atoms are being powered and charged and fired up by gravity, atoms are gravity energised and powered, so gravity is an energy that norurishes matter, so gravity I believe to be source energy that actually sustains and feeds geometric matter. If there was no gravity and it was cut off then matter would not continue to be able to form to be able to even exist, there would be no physical form, no animated life, there would be no Sacred Geometric Matter the Sacred building blocks of the Scaffolding of Life.

So each particle of matter is really a wormhole, a whirlpool in a river of light, does the whirlpool or wormhole

have any substance, any existence, no it
does not, it is a whirlwind, a swirling of
counter current and counter flow, its a
vortex it has constant form, a pattern,
a shape, because the fluid energy that
is flowing through it is continuing to
flow the same way, that is what is
happening inside the structure of the
atom, that is the processes going on
inside the atom.

Now going back to the blackhole, the
white hole emerges out of the blackhole
in a circular sphere, this is what
energises or causes the nucleus, so the
atom is a miniture blackhole. So the
secret mystery of physics, atoms fuelled
by gravity or gravity nourishes and
sustains and actually feeds atoms, this
is Source energy. This energy fuels all
Universes, Galaxies, Solar Systems,
Planets, and the Avatars living entities
in a physical form as well as as all the
animals which are an expression of the
plants, all life. It flows into all life to
create form in all densities of physical

realities, it flows into create and allow the processes of the Scaffolding of Life, the building blocks of Geometric Matter, fuelled by Spirit energy, by Source energy, energy of the Sacred, energy of the Eternal, the energy of Immortality, just like you and me in Human Avatar form, then on a path of enlightenment we start remembering waking up and raise our Consciousness and perceiving our core, to our true nature, our essence, and that we can grow a new body with our Consciousness by tapping into the Blueprint with our DNA of the Schematics of a Diamond Sun Light Body, by accessing our Luminous Energy Fields around our Avatars, our Human bodies, the Software that informs the Hardware the DNA to grow the manifested body and we can stop the cycles of life and death, we can evolve and quantum leap to a Luminous Angelic Light being becoming an embodied Immortal, for Eternal we will once again be, enlightened at one with all existence, I just love it, how awesome is the ascension process it's just magical in wonder and magial in nature.

Before we touched on the ten fold rate between the weak and the strong nucleus that is geometric, as the strong nucleus is exactly ten times more powerful than the weak nucleus and remember gravity energy, source energy is flowing in at a rate of ten meter by ten squared and when you transverse and move through that energy, it has a force of resistance, it propels against you, so this causes inertia the directional movement, so force like if you push hard on a motor bikes brakes and you move forwards as you move through gravity energy. So you have a push of gravity, as gravity is energy that is forcing us downwards, from the outside going inside.

Now inside the atom we also have a charge which is the physical properties of magical geometric matter, that causes it to experience a force when in an electromagnetic field, the two types of electrical charge positive and negative, referred to and carried by protons and electrons, the proton has a charge of plus (+e) and the electron has a charge of minus (-e). So it is important to focus the mind on silence, stillness to control the emotional body the emotional state to be able to vibrate on a positive charge to fire up and continually fuel your photons, to raise Consciousness, and access your Schematic Blueprint within your DNA, to grow a body of light and ascend to return home, to your natural state of a Rainbow Light being, an Angel of Spirit, connected to all that be in the Creation, but right now you are masquerading as and are an Individual playing a singular cell, a charcter on a stage of light energy and me in the present I play lovelifelee, but awakened to my core of an Immortal Eternal Rainbow being of Ultra Violet Source energetic Consciousness, the force of gravity, the energetic Light force of Source energy.

So there is a charge in the nucleus, positive or negative, an electrical charge in the electrons, so gravity is powering the atom and the atom has movement a flow of charge, moving between negative to positive, so creating a strong enough electrical charge movement a flow of energy. You create a gravitational thrust, a push of energy that propels in a direction, a field of electro gravity, that creates gravitational movement of thrust. The nucleus of the atom and that of flow, creates gravitation versions of the same field, creating and performing the same execution, doing the same thing.

So now moving onto the geometric pyramid shape to understand why pyramids work at fifty two degrees and the more powerful seventy two degree pyramids, which is twenty times more powerful than the fifty two degree pyramid. The pyramid shape formed at fifty two degrees or at seventy two degrees is able to capture the energy, that is flowing into the Earth and then leave the Earths surface and the pyramids harness that energy and it is fluid like, so it flows and can swirl and spin creating currents that are the Earth, your body, the Planets, the Stars, the Solar Systems, the Galaxies, the Universes, all have a Torus field around them and through them a constant flow of energy on the large scales of the atom, its just many atoms joined as One, United.

So our bodies has this constant flow of energy coming in, flowing inside, but also flowing outside, its like a bird being blown in the opposite direction its flying by an invisible force, the force of gravity the force of source. Its fluid energy doing this on the micro level its powdered light energy. So the swirl the spin in a gravitational field, its spinning and when you take the form or shape of a funnel shape like the pyramid and build it out of natural materials like stone, quartz, copper, gold, silver, this fluid energy will not flow in from all directions all sides, it will channel one direction from the large end to the small end of the pyramid shape structure, this creates a vortex flow, the same as when water goes down a sink hole with water in it, it is moving through it at a particular rate, a flow creating the vortex flow of energy, and the pyramid shapes are named after the house of energy also known as the fuel in the middle or fire in the middle, the energy centre.

This then moves onto form power or shape power a capacity to hold energy, creating a built up force or flow of force energy, creating potential, a different perspective, a developing capacity, in our human experience, and situation, an unrealized potential, of our birth right of tapping into Source energy, via our Blueprint in our DNA, through Conscious thought, creating Sacred Geometric Matter and evolving back to our true nature of an Angelic Eternal Light being, manifesting physical Creation with our every thought. So be careful, be mindful, find silence, peace, tranquillity and project Inner peace outward, creating peace in all directions of the Hyper-Dimensional Matrix and Creation, this will therefore ignite your enlightenment, for we are all one, in service to all in the Oneness that exists, that be, in the Brahman the Whole.

Its just magical in nature, magical in Spirit, its light energy on the vibration of love, pure Ultra Violet energetic Consciousness, in its highest form state, our true nature. The forces and energy that fuel and fire the Scaffolding of Life, which is Sacred Geometric Matter the building blocks of Life, of all physical form, osilating, contracting, expanding, vibrating, creating multiple densities of realities for us to manifest into to grow Spiritually. The main point of it all the lessons we learn as we continually grow and evolve Spiritually, so we can Create and Co-Create wonder, beauty and magic in physical forms, eternally expressing Consciousness of energetic light, vibrating osilating in its essence, the essence of Spirit.

Torsion fields are generated by distorting the geometry and space its self of the geometric matter the building blocks of life, the scaffolding of form creating physical matter realities. As when geometry is distorted you create currents objects with a certain surface of geometry that will simultaneously, at the same time generate, right and left torsion fields of a certain form, shape, configuration, depending on the geometry of the object. So a left torsion field means it will spin to the left direction, and the right torsion field will spin to the right direction. So a torus field, a donught shape, a continual flow of energy in the torus field configuration. So anti clockwise one way and clockwise rotation on the other side. So there is a constant force of energy pushing down and pushing up, so pyramid shapes harness levity force, the upward push of force which is fluid, even powdered light. Also inside the dodecahedron multi dimensional structure there is a tetrahedron, spinning a hundred and twenty different patterns that create a hundred and twenty proteins, the tetrahedrons, which is two pyramids and the larger bottom the base is connected base to base, with these forces of fluid energy moving through them, this is source energy in a funnel spinning, creating energy, power, fuel, fire, so creating manifestation of creational form, creating part of the Scaffolding of Life, the wonderful World of Geometric Matter, its awesome, don't you just love the magic and wonder of it all, its spectacular to see from the eyes of the heart, for blessed we truly be.

The physics of the nucleus apply that to the outer layer of the atom its fluid, look at the physics of the blackhole and apply that physics to the nucleus of the atoms. The blackhole has a boundry all around it, it is enveloped and called the event horizon, when you can cross the event horizon, then your whole understanding of physics changes, matter compresses and the flow of time changes and the event horizon boundry changes and a blackhole is a gravitational vortex, so the event horizon is called the Scwarzchild radius, which means and represents the thickness or depth of the boundry around the event horizon that is around the blackhole, that creates the gravitational pull that the blackhole is creating. So the size of the event horizon will be a three dimensional hole which is round and spherical in shape, in nature. So a spherical hole with a certain radius called a

Schwarzchild radius.
The math that creates this form the Schwarzchild proton of the blackhole was reapplied to the nucleus and atom, they behave one and the same way, act the same, the atomic nucleus and blackhole are the same, so the nucleus of an atom is a blackhole, it really actually is. Just as stars do having energy flowing in and out of them at the same time, the torus energy field that powers all atoms and mass of connected atoms, this flow in and out creating a visible light. So we can now see we have to change our opinions and views on how atoms are created how they are manifested into form, this takes us back to the mathematical construct of the strong force, created to explain how protons and the nucleus of the atom hold and connect together, what a wonderful World of Geometric osilating magical Matter, the Sacred building blocks of the Scaffolding of Life, magical in nature, in Spirit, in the Eternal and in the Divine.

The Chakra System Activating The Pineal Gland To Access The Angelic Human Light Body

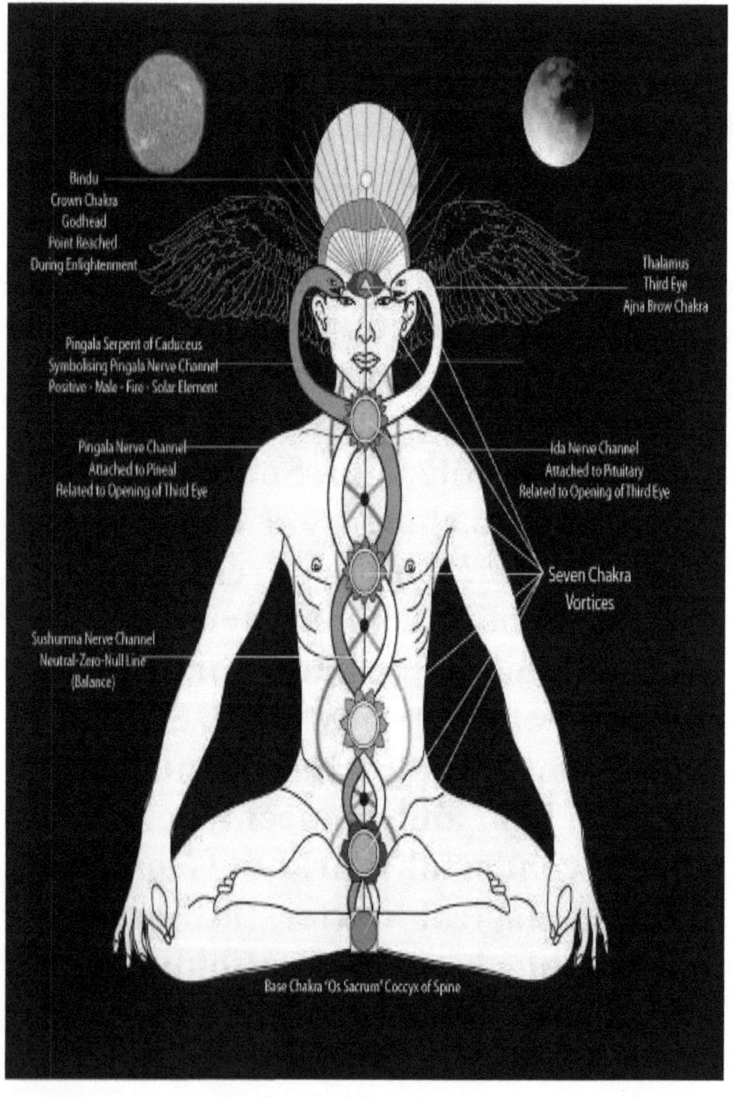

CHAPTER NINE

DNA Biotechnology & Its Symbiotic Relationship To The Essence Of Spirit & The Diamond Sun Body

One night after a Shamanic ceremony I gazed up into the Cosmos and I thought of all the trillions of species and races of life in all the trillions of Galaxies in all the Multi Cosmoses of the Creation and started smiling, because really it seems so complicated and complex this advanced DNA Biotechnology and its symbiotic relationship to the essence of Eternal Spirit. But really if you can learn to understand and comprehend with clarity the quantum mechanics and its processes, and the energetic forces and

229

there processes of this DNA advanced Biotechnology, then you start to perceive the essence of Spirit and its energetic processes, its then actually quite simpler than one would have thought to actually crack the codes of this Multidimensional Multi-layered puzzle of animated Life of DNA advanced Biotechnology. Especially once you have raised your Consciousness and started Consciously interacting with your DNA, via upgrading your Luminous Energy field the Software that informs the DNA Hardware, and doing this in a ceremonial fashion with the element of fire, using and accessing your Sacred Chi Life Force, the energy of Spirit. How awesome when it becomes clearer and vivid that the illusion of physical reality is an awesome hologram of the Minds construct via our Eternal Spirit Consciousness.

The human mind believing in the Minds illusionary constructs because you are lost in thoughts, so if you lose the thoughts you will see all dimensions of existence, and if you wish this then command it so with your intentions and you shall humbly make it so, this then allows you to gain more access of the possibilities of experience, energetically, physically, and Spiritually.

We have to access all of this Consciously and via diet and learn to use this Sacred Geometry living science and create a peaceful and beautiful World of abundance, for our children's, children's, children.

Then when we go in the Mind and perceive Time with clarity, we come to the realization that time does not exist, only the present now exists thats why other races came back in time and folded in from other dimensions, to tell us if you carry on with nuclear technologies and War, some of these other races from the future would not exist because we are all connected on so many levels, but we know we've turned a corner and we will evolve on a positive timeline, if you Consciously manifest this through the electromagnetic fields of the Planet and the Creation.

So some Souls will not be graduating from this Karmic cycle and will come back to another three dimensional reality to learn from past mistakes of there repetitive cycles or Service to Self actions for another twenty six thousand plus years in another Planetary cycle. Others will evolve to the fifth dimensional reality to live a fifth dimensional way of being, and a smaller group on Planet Earth will evolve to Homo-Luminous being fully embodied able to transcend time and space able to reside outside of liner time and space in the Immortal realms, in the Kingdoms of Heaven, in the Kingdoms of Light. They will and I am also manifesting this for myself and others in the Oneness of all that is, to quantum leap ten thousands years into the future, like my future self is reaching out, arms stretched, palms open to pull me into who I am to become, who I am becoming an Angelic Divine Human Light being manifesting from Source Ultra Violet light waves of energy, in powdered light form. Creating all from love and light, with compassion and empathy, my true nature of an Immortal Interdimensional Light being of Conscious energy, by Divine decree in the Oneness of all of Creation, for we are all One, in the highest vibratory energy waves of Violet light, of Co-Creative Consciousness, Spirit beings we be, you and me, just disconnected temporarily to have Individual experiences to grow mentally, emotionally, physically, and ultimately Spiritually.

So the concept of time was made up to survive and reference our surrounding reality, in this three dimensional reality of matter, there are many different dimensions in each density level, and we are learning to grow and travel and transverse Interdimensionally.

So when we come into a Conscious state of contemplation, we can perceive that an atom has a nucleus in the center with the electrons around it and inside is 999.999 space as it flashes light, and our Human Avatars biological cells flash a hundred Herz a second, so flashes light a hundred times a second, so this Universe and the whole Creation is a projected light hologram of animated physical form that creates our surrounding realities, including our animated physical biological Avatars, that is all created by and encompassed by the super advanced Biotechnology of DNA. So the atoms nucleus is in the center with the electrons around it and inside is so much space as it flashes light a hundred times a second, so because this is a hologram that is why there is so much space. I find many people find it hard to see past there physical bodies and the nutriants they feed it, let alone the levels of science and depths of spirit and the energies that are fundamental to allow this Creation to be in existence, that of electromagnetism, the strong and weak nuclear forces and gravity, the energy of Spirit. When we focus our mental energy on understanding the Creation in our Mind we start to perceive and understand this super advanced DNA Biotechnology, which allows us Eternal Spirits to become animated in physical form, we can then percieve this clearer knowing some of the history of the Founder Christos Races with a much clearer point of view, with a sense of clarity, about how Spirit, the Eternal Source Ultra Violet Divine energetic Consciousness, operates this advanced DNA holographical Biotechnology, with a much clearer understanding of the essence of energetic Spirit.

So now going back to the Founder Christos Races from which our genetics were created from, and perceiving our genetic ancestors known as the Oraphim, they are of Blue Ray Consciousness they are the Cosmic parents of the Indigo Races and are accessible and able to fully support the incarnated Indigo Races presently at this time, also these Energetic Unity Field Blue Ray Races have been introduced by way of the Thirteenth Gate circuits of Mother Arc Aqua Ray frequency that's reconnected into our Planetary grid system and its holographical Matrix field. The Blue Ray Race have also been able to connect to this plane of existence and have returned claim of this domain in the Natural Laws of the Creator. The Collective of the Blue Ray is of Four Universal Harmonic Layers of the Families of Blue Ray Consciousness, there are Three Primal Order Sound Fields, the Threefold Founder Flame that make up the Ray Aspects of our

Universal Creation and the Blue Ray is of the First Order of instant emanation of the Source emission of the Mother Arc Aqua Ray frequency. The Highest Order of the Blue Ray Family Source emanate from the Thirteenth Circuitry Gate which is the first layer projected from the Zero Point Gravity Field, the Universal Creator Core. The First Order Blue Ray Family is the Esoteric One Hundred and Forty Five Thousand Genetic Timekeepers of our Universal System, they were also known as the Code of the Blue Nile in ancient Sirian and Egyptian texts.

It is so fascinating because that means that our ancestors the Oraphim are a part of the Diamond Sun DNA Christos Bloodline Lineages, the absolute Original Humans created from the Founder Race Bloodlines, the Diamond Sun refers to the Original Blueprint design of the Angelic Human Twelve Strand DNA Silicate Matrix, this was the potential DNA and higher Consciousness experienced by Angelic

Humans in past ancient time cycles in the Fifth Dimensional parallel Earth, that was before it had a catastrophic upheaval.

So this is so exciting where we learn about our future potential because the Original Founder Oraphim schematic Avatar design, which is also known as the Double Diamond Sun Body, has the design of a fully embodied Twelve Stranded DNA and has further access to Twenty Four other Dimensions of Consciousness while manifested in a Human physical Avatar body, this implies with meaning that the Oraphim DNA at full potential when it is activated allows for the Immortality of the physical Human Avatar and the ability for the Consciousness bodies full transmutation out of the Holographical Dimensional Time Matrix, accessing the Eternal Spirit realms. Our DNA also allows us to heal and restore the fragmented electromagnetic fields of the Planet and the Universe, so we are very powerful Spiritual Human Light beings with unique highly genetically advanced DNA.

Then with contemplation on Universal history we can perceive that the First Primal Order Sound field of Universal Creation in our Light Time Matrix that is the Blue Ray, the Second Primal Order Sound field is the Gold Ray and the Third Primal Order Sound field is the Violet Ray. So the tone translation of the Blue Ray level of our Source Field is Melchizedek, so the Blue Ray is part of the Threefold Founder Flame and Cosmic Triad, it was distorted until Mother Arc Aqua Ray frequency was able to return to the Earth core and reclaim the Blue Ray out of the Fallen Melchizedek's control.
We can also get more understanding when we perceive Universal history of the Interdimensional Association of Free Worlds and there Task Force known as the Guardian Alliance Organization that specializes in propagation of the Emerald Covenant

that serves as the governing body of a super huge Collective of Interdimensional Intergalactic Guardian Angelic Star League Nations. So through the Creation of the Guardian Alliance over Five Hundred and Sixty Nine million years ago the vast array of Star League Nations from Galaxies in Densities One through to Four in Dimensions One to Twelve, were brought into an organized and Co-Supportive communications and extremely vast resource network, with the Guardian Alliance operating under the contolled direction and guidance of the Melchizedek Cloister Eieyani Master Council, the Yanas Ascended Masters, the Emerald Order Elohei Elohim, Founder Races and the Interdimensional Association of Free Worlds, under there directed guidance are the Guardian Alliance of Twelve smaller Seal Signet Councils with Authority composed of representatives of various Star League Nations that were formed, each of the Twelve Seal

Signet Councils of the Guardian Alliance were appointed by the Fifth Density Melchizedek Cloister Eieyani Master Council and serves as the Primary Guardians of One of the Twelve Primary Star Gates in the Universal Templar Complex of our Time Matrix, of this Super Advanced Holographical DNA Biotechnology. These Founder Races and different genetic groups of different Nations all work for the Service of Others Ideology in alignment with the Law of One Ideology of Christos Consciousness and for the continued protection and restoration within our Light Time Matrix. On the Dark side you have the Fallen Angel Races and there genetic off spring that want to dominate and have absolute total control of this Universal Light Time Matrix and that of all the Multiverses in this Cosmoses Light Time Matrix. So with this information of these Universal bloodline lineages genetic knowledge, and Universal Ancient history, it gives us an overview of who we are as a species as a race, and where we have come from in the Cosmic genetic pool, and what we were created for in this Light Time Matrix, to repair the interity of the Creations Fractal Electromagnetic fields and to be able to Ascend beyond the Hyper-Dimensional Matrix, to potentially evolve into by accessing our Luminous Schematic Blueprint within our Luminous Software Energy Fields and rewrite our DNA codes to grow a new physical Avatar body that lives, dies and heals differently, stepping into who we are Eternally becoming, which is Immortal Angelic Source Light beings, with their Diamond Sun Body Activated.

CHAPTER TEN

The Sacred Geometric Building Blocks Of The Scaffolding Of Life & Conscious Evolution

If we go into Conscious Awareness in the Mind on the subject of the hidden knowledge of the Scaffolding of Life, the Scaffolding of Life is this in simple terms – energy plus vibration equals matter, seeing is energy and speaking is vibration, which creates geometry of living matter (the building blocks of the cells that build the Scaffolding of Life), so thoughts plus voice equals physical reality.

So all that really exists in this photon, one particle of light known as the Universe, is light in all spectrums of colours of the rainbow, which vibtrates at different frequencies, creating different densities of matter, different realities physical and non-physical for us to experience and grow Spiritually and to express ourselfs in different forms, different Avatars, not always Human form, we are are billions and billions of years old, we have been around for eons and eons, we have already manifested and experienced all forms of bipedal life and energetic forms of life, in all different realities in this Universe, and all over the Cosmoses of Multiverses and beyond outside of linear time in the Eternal Spirit Realms of the Kingdoms of Light.

So Consciousness equals light, light at resonance in vibration creates matter, Sacred Geometry, so then imagine a dodecahedron and the corners of the dodecahedron are were the amino acids are symbiotic and that the corners are the only solid to the dodecahedron structure and inside the dodecahedron is a tetrahedron and the same again its the corners that are the only solid of the structure that are fed by proteins and inside the rotating tetrahedron there is 120 different patterned ways the Torus field inside can rotate and spin, which will then create 120 different protiens to create different avatar biological structures, even smaller on the micron level if we go inside it becomes a refractual pattern and actually refractruals down to Infinitly.

So much information in one single cell of the Universe, because the Universe can be created again in it's entirety from One cell of the Universe, One single particle of light amazing, mind blowing, awesome, just magical and Divine in nature. So if you go back to the dodecahedron and imagine a tower block of them stacked on top of each other, then you can see by Divine Universal design that DNA is attracted to the tower block of crystal structured dodecahedrons and then DNA spirals around and starts to form biological structure, biological forms, solid and non solid.

So my advice to all on Planet Earth is study this and start to manipulate matter Consciously from the Heart through your Hearts Electromagnetic field and work on meditation in joint groups, the larger the more powerful to manifest matter quicker to get a desired outcome, and then as group changing your reality around you. If millions of people United meditating and visualized all the other people of the Worlds Nations in there entirity of millions and millions and millions, connecting to the Planets electromagnetic field it would amplify others to become aware of whats happening in reality around them to change our surrounding, encompassing reality by connecting while manifesting in Unifed meditation.

The citizens awake do not believe the false narratives around them, that are pushed by negative agendas and negative beings that are lost in the Maya of there Minds, they are inflicting unnecassary human suffering that is coming from them that have lost their Divine spark of Light within, its faded, dwindling causing them to create a dark reality upon others for their own selfish gain, and for other negative races and entities agendas, they will be vanquished and so defeated and dispelled to be scattered to be dispersed back to the Source field.

APATHEOSIS means the highest point in the development of something, an example is the culmination or climax. APATHIOSUS means man becomes God, meaning someone who reaches Divine status, Divination.

You are creating the geometry of this World with the power of your

consciousness and intention, you need
to realize that you are making a direct
interconnected powerful impact in to
our co-creative enveloping reality.
One must learn that focusing your
attention on something is a creative
practice, because thoughts are
wavelengths that influence the
structure of a encompassing reality.
Therefore you must raise your focused
attention and individual awareness,
and be intentional in your conscious
thoughts, with focused awareness of
what you are thinking, by having good
thoughts, constructive thoughts, to
manifest into the co-creative collective
fields of this World, to create a
peaceful encompassing environment.
So move into your heart space and
have hope for the future, and stay
positive, while creating abundance,
harmony, and unity for all as a
collective. Let's set aside the low
vibration of fear, and step into a new
way of expression, creating a new way
to experience, creating an evolution of

a new way of being, a new way of existing.
Everything starts with the understanding that you are a powerful conscious being, and everything you intend will become your reality, because Creation is built on the wavelength of consciousness.

The physical Human being manifested on Planet Earth is to complete their karmatic cycle and evolve to open their Rainbow body of Light, ending a cycle to become Ascended, which is being in the body fully incarnated in physical form and in a constant love vibration, living on Planet Earth in the fifth dimension, but also accessing all dimensions of realty in Creation.

We have a moral peril to take meditative action in thought, visualization and manifestation to combat immediately the negative agendas, and to manifest in groups of eight and more because in groups of people the power is more focused in on the intention, and then by the group visualizing and then feeling the outcome in these groups, this then creates larger energetic waves of frequency vibration and is then manifested as matter in the form of Sacred Geometry into the Creation. Then as we are creating vibration this means we are effecting each other as we directly effect each others moods, behaviours, feelings, from the ether with that of our electromagnetic energetic environment, which some people have lost touch with, so we need to reconnect to nature, and Spirit, meditate, visualize the outcome and feel the outcome, have love in our hearts, connect our minds and hearts as one and diet is key to raising the bodies vibration, remember the second coming is you and me, it is us, each person, each Soul ready to Ascend to evolve and graduate from the third dimensional reality of experience and move onto another experience of expression in a higher vibrational frequency of reality.

Don't forget how powerful you are individually, that you with your individual light energetic Consciousness, that makes your light vibrate at a frequency of sound resonance, and with that created matter in the form of Sacred Geometry, creating physical form, creating biological Avatars, the body in which you reside right now in the present, this body is enveloped in a Luminous Energy field around you. You are Gods and Goddesses beings of Light from the Kingdom of Light, you create your own reality around you, making it from the Sacred Geometry of the Scaffolding of all Life in the Universe.
So us United as Gods and Godesses beings of Light, we can dispel the negative almost instantly immediately if we are One Mind, Co-Creating

Collectively, with the resonance of the matter we manifest into being.
And by using scaler waves when in danger only, to defend ones self or others. An example how powerful scaler waves are is when a psychic gentleman took twelve psychic children over to Africa, they joined hands all thirteen of them united in intention and sent scaler waves outwards to a village of negative extraterrestrials wiping them out instantly.
Remember how powerful you truly be an example is that it takes three Souls to create a life a feminine energy joined with a masculine energy and the Soul manifesting in, so it takes three Souls to create life but the same three Souls can Co-Create an entire Solar System as all is possible, so imagine what millions of us can manifest with pure intention, with all possabilities that can and are unfolding, wish blessings to all and stand in your Eternal inner Chi Power, access your manifesting gifts that are your birth right, access your

Rainbow Diamond Sun Body of Light
and Ascend, transcend, transverse the
Hyper-Dimensional Matrix of Light, of
Spirit energy, of the Sacred, of the
Divine Source gravity energy.
Lets pull ourselfs into who we are
becoming Individually and Co-
Collectivly, lets pull the whole Human
race into its becoming and quantum
leap ten thousand years into our
manifested becoming. There is much to
ponder on for this to come into fruition
in all the possibilities of future
timelines.

I wish all Sentient life well with a
Namaste and Eternal blessings, be kind
to yourselfs on your enlightenment
path, but be disiplined with
concentrado because it is the key of
Mediation and Diet, to then be able to
then access the Blueprint Schematics
within your Luminous Energy field,
then able to rewrite and program your
DNA, and then Consciously manifest to
evolve to metamorphosis, as is your

Divine right by accessing your
Rainbow Diamond Sun Body of Light.
Manifesting by saying, with the Divine
power in me, I choose to manifest my
Eternal Diamond Sun Light Body by
activating all twelve strands of DNA
Consciously and to make it so and so it
shall be, and so it shall be. For truly we
are in Service of the Oneness, for that
is all there truly be, the essense of
Eternal Spirit.

I see humanity connecting, Unifing,
Uniting as a Collective of Co-Creative
Consciousness in this great Awakening,
as we come together for the Ascension,
because for the Ones with an open
Heart can access all the possibilities
that are waiting for us to manifest into
being, into majestic form, creating
mulitidimensionally with beauty and
wonder from different densities of
light.
I see the inevitable outcome that we
will be called upon by the free will
choices of many Human Souls that are

of the negative agendas, called to ceremony to dispel, so that there is nothing for Archons, the Jinn to feed on, so that the Archons cease to exist. So Souls that are free that can perceive behind the veil and are waking, becoming Conscious, tapping into their multidimensional Consciousness, perceiving the illusions of deception, percieving some have been trapped here for some time. Be under no illusion, some highly advanced Spiritual beings have also been trapped in this Arcaic system, and some have been trapped in this incarnation cycle, that was created on one level to enslave races but also for the the purpose of us to move beyond the cycle of necessity, for the good of our Souls growth and past the manipulations that slow our growth while we are waking up to who we truly are Individually and Collectively, to remembering our Eternal nature. So the time is now, the opportunity presents itself in the present, or others can stay in the 3rd

dimension for another 26000 plus year cycle on another three dimensional Planet, for more three dimensional experience and Spiritual growth. Not me I wish to check out to another experience. But we are now able to avoid those cycles then being able to come into a new way of being ending the Soul contract of a 26000 plus years in this cycle and then able to Ascend and even transend. Because now the energetic wave of Ascention have returned via the the blackhole in the centre of the Milky Way, taking 26000 plus years to return back to the Planet, this now allows the portholes to open around us on the Planet this then allows us to graduate, for us to access them, to Ascend to a higher dimension of reality even to transend and quantum leap ten thousand years into the Eternal pure Illuminated nature of the Homo-Luminous Light Beings we be, for Divine Source field Spirit beings we truly be.

Be true to yourself have pure intentions for Yourself, the Collective and the Creation, from an open heart and all will fall into place in every step you take while creating and manifesting Matter, into biological form into the Creation, and you will be blessed, this is the way of being, all is based on a Universal Cosmic understanding of Morality, then from compassion and empathy, all magic is truly created from the Eternal by the Oneness of Creation, from the Source field of Spirit.

So Spiritual practices this is to include Shamanism which is the Original Spiritual practice of the Universe, because Shamanic practices use the language of DNA via the communication of song and of imagery via Spirit. This is also told to us in scriptures or passed down by oral traditions, they tell us to have love in our hearts, honor and to respect ourselfs and our neighbours and then you shall find the light and enter the kingdom of heaven.

What this actually means is, (you shall find the light and enter the kingdom of heaven) is that – Our DNA flashes a 100Hz a second, our DNA flashes light a hundred times a second, every cell of your body is flashing light, vibrating at frequency, and you have a Luminous Energy field around the Human Avatar, the Human biological body. So you have a Luminous Energy field around your Avatar, that envolopes your biological physical body, that is a foot above your head, a foot below your feet and stretches outwards as far as your arms can stretch outwards, the Luminous Energy field that envelopes your physical body, it organises the body, for example if you have a glass table top and you place metal iron filings on the glass top and place a magnet underneath, the metal filings are attracted to the magnet and create form, a shape connected together to create one iron file body.

The Luminous Energy Field is the software that informs tree hardware the DNA to grow the Human biological body, you are not the mind or body, you are Eternal Ultra Violet energetic Consciousness also known as Spirit.
The hardware the DNA manifactures the physical body, when we download the latest version of the software, by reaching into the future and stepping into who we are becoming, then we can receive the instructions that will reprogramme our DNA, that then helps us to create new bodies that age differently, die differently, and heal differently.
To do this we have to raise our bodies vibration, coming from the heart, with love in our hearts and eating a high vibrational vegetarian diet, with meditation, prayer and other ancient disiplines like yoga, Tai-Chi, Qigong, martial arts, reki and other energy disciplines, and by partaking in diets and also by ingesting trees and plants and by fasting.

The path of Spirituality is one of teacher and student and even the teacher is a student as the student then becomes a teacher, they will be learning from the student, so when learning we must always remember to be humble as we learn and grow with knowledge and wisdom and raise our Consciousness to evolve on the path of enlightenment and Ascension.
So contemplating on Shamanism you realise an accomplished Shaman in ceremonies is actually able to hold Sacred Space, so that the other participants recognize their own authentic potency, there own essential power within that is in us all, the Divine Power of Spirit.

So when scripture says you will find the light, it means you can open and access your Diamond Sun Light Body, stop the cycles of life and death, stopping your karmatic cycles of reincarnation. This will bring you back to your true nature of an Eternal

Interdimensional Light being of Conscious energy, no longer separated from the Universe you are able to travel in the Hyper-Dimensional Matrix of all dimensions and realities, you then are living being fully embodied in the 5th dimensional earth reality, but able to leave your body at will or travel with your body in a sixty foot field of light by travelling through the portholes connected to the Suns, Sun to Sun, Solar System to Solar System, Galaxy to Galaxy, or you can just teleport when you can comprehend and understand that you are powdered light, which is the micron scale of light beyond the perception of light waves. So we are Immortal Interdimensional Source field Light beings of Conscious energy, we flash DNA to create different looking bodies, different species and races, and in the now different Human bodies, to have different Human experiences, of different races, with different beliefs in religions, and live in different Cultures

and Societies, to grow Spiritually and
pay past karma off from past
incarnations.
So the Universe is One photon, One
particle of light refracting down to
Galaxies and Solar Systems and
Planets and biological life, so the
Universe and our physical bodies are
flashing light at different frequencies of
vibrations at different densities. We
are all one family of light in the Whole
Creation, the Brahman, the Whole.

So we reside and live in a physical body
and Universe made of flashing
vibrating light in a holographical
Universe of Light, we are all one family
of Light in the Creation. Ancient
knowledge and Spiritual practices
teach us we are Spirit, to live by way
and in harmony with nature, never
take more than is needed to keep the
Eternal balance.
Your Luminous Blueprint Energy field
Schematics can be accessed through
your DNA, the part of the DNA the

main stream science call JUNK DNA but it is not, it's a lie, there is a Schematic Blueprint within the non-junk DNA to grow a Luminous Light Body, allowing you to stop the cycles of life and death and evolve from Homo-Sapian to Homo-Luminous, allowing you to Ascend, meaning being in your body fully (embodied) but also able to access all dimensions of reality in this Universe and the Multiverses, accessing the Hyper-Dimensional Matrix of Life, of existence.

Now the secret truth on the Spiritual level of understanding is that they the dark forces are trying to stop you opening your Light Body, to stop you opening your Luminous Energy fields and stop you from Ascending and evolving to Homo-Luminous. The Dark forces are with these Biological Weapon Vaccines trying to damage your RNA the building blocks of your DNA, so you cannot access the Blueprint in your DNA with the informational plans and Schematics to design your Eternal Diamond Sun Light Body, because these Bioweapons are altering your RNA the building blocks of your DNA to stop you from opening your Diamond Sun Light Bodies, to stop you Ascending and travelling in the Hyper-Dimensional Light Time Matrix made up of all densities and dimensions of all realites. Within your DNA are the instructions of a Blueprint to grow a new body that lives differently, dies differently and heals differently, the Blueprint of a Homo-Luminous body of Light, is accessed through a diet of plants that are high vibrational and through meditation and ceremonies, along with many other ancient practices and disiplines.

You can grow the Luminous Light Body energetically by tranfer and Consciously with your Mind the tool of the Avatar, with silence and stillness that is part of the key and also with a strict diet this then allows you to gain access to your Kundalini Energy Systems, then you will be able to stand in your Eternal Power and then you will be able to experience your gifts, strengths, and abilities and utilize your Eternal Chi Power, that is your Spiritual Power.

The Creator of Light that's you and me, gave us free will, by Divine decree, no Government, Corporation, religion, Elite Extraterrestrial blood cult, no ethenic group has the right to tell you how to live on Planet Earth, so long as you follow the ten commandments and Universal law, live in peace, love thy neighbour, be treated as you wish to be treated, with logic and common sense really, and when you are standing in your Eternal Chi Power you can circumnavigate around and beyond the illusions of the negative systems and structures in place, moving beyond the tiny illusionary Matrix of reality that was created to control and suppress you.

Namaste I wish all beings in Creation and on Planet Earth to have inner peace to project outer peace, to attain enlightenment to not suffer with sorrow to be lead from Mortality to Immortality, to see the Illusion that surrounds them, I wish you all Consciousness, to raise your embodied Avatar biological bodies vibration and for your to Ascend, then access and travel the Creation, in the Cosmos in its entirety, for you and me we be Angels, do you see, Light beings, Interdimensional beings, Eternal beings maninfesting from Divine Ultra Violet Source energetic Consciousness, known also as Spirit, the essence of the Divine, so blessings on your Earth walk of Life and on your journey home to the Kingdoms of Light via Ascension, then transcending to all your potential can be, illuminated once more in your true Eternal nature, Namaste LoveLifeLee.

CHAPTER ELEVEN

The Psychic Childs Connection To Their Star Family & Download Data Received

& The Purpose & The Science Of Soul Evolution

First lets discuss the Worlds militaries who observe and conduct tests on the psychic children of the World, these World wide militaries are controlled by corrupt criminal families, who deem the psychic children as a threat to their domination of power. Then if we look at the militaries and intelligence agencies of the World that have teachers in schools to observe the school children to see if they have psychic abilities, and if they they report it and the children are taken into secret military, intelligence, and secret space programs. In China the governments military around sixteen years ago were studying the psychic children with the scientific community, as they studied these super psychic children for around ten years, then they got scared, very scared of these super psychic children because they realized that they were so powerful that they decided through fear to control them, because they found some could walk through walls by resonating their body's frequency to the vibration of the physical matter that they wanted to pass through, and so they started rounding them up and arresting them and imprisoning them. They even went after the powerful chi martial arts masters and practitioners that practiced Qigong, Falun Gong, and other chi energy martial arts masters. If you look at China history when in the past the more conservative party was in power they promoted the Falun

Gong practice for health to save the Government money on health costs and for the benefit of society, and you saw every day all over China in the parks hundreds and thousands of thousands of citizens doing their daily practice together, it was all ages and generations. Then when the communist Government came to power they realized they may not be able to control the citizens if they had access to their core chi energy power and psychic abilities, so they suppressed this practice as illegal and ordered all practioners to sign a form saying it was a false teaching and that they denounced the practice, but most of then around one billion citizens refused and over the years were rounded up and put into detainment camps, where they are used by the Government in their organ harvesting program, which sells organs to order from live prisoners, which are then murdered for their organs. China's criminal organ harvesting program is the largest in the World, it's a tragedy to the innocent citizens, and considered mass murder, genocide, and crimes against humanity. The reason that the Chinese Government military did this is because they realized the chi masters and psychic childrens true psychic potential, the potential core chi energy power that they pocessed, and they realized that these psychic children could at will wipe out the entire Chinese military in any given moment if they chose to do so. So the Chinese and other World militaries are trying to stop the psychic abilities of children everywhere but they cant really stop this evolution process, only hinder it. But when the military were studying this psychic children they realized something very important, because they found that when these children were around five, six, and seven years old, they themselves became aware of their psychic abilities. I believe this is when their Star families are communicating psychically and giving them downloads of information, for their mission on the Planet in their life time. Then the militaries realized that when these psychic children reach teenage years and hit puperty that their psychic abilities got stronger and stronger with the ability to focus that super strong psychic power. At this teenage puperty stage they found only one or two things occurred, they got more powerful or they lost their psychic abilities because they shut off, and the military could not understand or figure out why it happened, but they worked out the percentage of how many of these psychic teenagers were losing theie psychic abilities and it was around eighty percent that lost their powers. But the remaning twenty percent of the psychic children just got stronger and stronger in their psychic abilities to become super powerful human beings. The military in the USA also discovered that eighty percent of these gifted children reaching teenage puberty started to grown a calcium shield around the pineal gland, you can perceive this like an oyster shell around the pineal gland. This blocks the connection to the electromagnetic field around us in our encompassing environment stopping our connection to the Universe and our psychic communication with our Star families from previous incarnations.

Many children on Planet Gaia at a young age of around five to seven years old are becoming aware and conscious of other beings around them, some are energetic spiritual beings, some are extraterrestrials from their soul group races from previous incarnations in other Star Systems, others are negative races that appear benevolent but are just interested in the childs genetic DNA material for their hybrid breeding programs to advance their own species genetically. Some of these children being visited then inform their parents or guardians that they are not from this Planet, that they actually come from another Planet, many of these parents or guardians then ask the child well how did you come to be here on this Planet, these parents or guardians usually ask this with a bit of astonishment and laughter or jest with a playful or in frivoious mood or manner. But most of these children answer in a direct serious manner that surprises the adults, especially when a child responds, telling them that they teleported into their mothers womb, its at that moment that the adults become wide eyed and takes the child seriously and listen to what the child is expressing to them, because the child is seriously convinced this is their recollected memories of their personal experience. Many of these children first become aware that they have psychic abilities and are able to communicate with other beings in dreams, and communicate with these beings psychically, and that they can also interact with these beings in physical form. These children become aware they are using their minds eye, many are told this information from the beings that are interacting and teaching them and giving the child downloads of information, which is a part of their soul contract. Many of these children are using their abilities of telekinesis which is the psychic ability allowing them to influence a physical system without physical contact or interaction, like moving an object with their mind making it lift off a table and float in the air across the room to them.

I know a friend that was doing this at the age of six or seven years old and she told me that she had to stop doing this in front of her parents because they became freaked even slightly scared of what she was doing because it was out of the parent comprehension of understanding. Other children can use their intuition to find and locate objects around them or at great distances. Other children have the ability to manipulate their encompassing environment like manipulating matter around them, even with the ability to effect a direct change of the weather around them. Some of these children also gain the ability to float, to levitate.

These children are having interactions with these extraterrestrial beings but they are not fearful of the beings because it feels normal to them, it feels familiar to them, so they are not scared or afraid of these beings. Some of the children have dreams of positive extraterrestrials from their past incarnations in other Star Systems of many different species and races. But some are dreaming of and interacting with light blue skinned beings, but as a young six or seven year old child they do not fully comprehend that they are extraterrestrials at that point in time when these beings are introducing themselves to the child, but the child does understand that they are from another Planet. The child usually does not interpret or comprehend that they are their Star family, but they become fascinated and can be obsessed by these experiences with these beings. These children having these types of interactions in dreams between five to seven years old then start to have telepathic interactions with these beings at around the ages of their teen years usually at about fifteen years old, because there is usually a period in the later years as a child before they get into their teenage years that communication is stopped for around five or six years and the child lives a normal life like any other child. Then when they are in their teenage years that's when many of these children are having psychic experiences but not communication with these beings, but then become conscious of their genetic hybrid nature, its then that they become consciously aware of their interactions with these other beings. In the teenage years they become aware of abduction experiences, that's when they start having communication

and visited experiences with these extra dimensional beings and start getting downloads of data, this is the pivotal point in their understanding and comprehension of their past experiences with these beings. These relationships with the beings and their downloads of information data are on subjects such as really complex physics and metaphysics, that are giving information of the metaphysics of the structure of existence, so data on the mechanics of consciousness.
Many of these children like many other children on the Planet like myself wanted to understand the physics of existence, this is why myself and other kids have been questioning the evolutionary existence of humanity, from a child perspective with information we were told as a child about humanities evolution like how we transitioned from lower apes into hominoid humans native to this Planet, that we evolved from monkey's into human beings, this did not make sense

to me, unless there was genetic manipulation through experiments. To me it made no sense and by the age of fifteen years old I understood that we were spirit beings manifesting into a human avatar for an experience. I also understood that we were in a Universe of multi species and races and that there were Universal wars going on between different species that were fighting over territories, minerals, and over genetics, that's when I realized that we were in a Universal Genetic Seed War, with other races manipulating other species of races to take or steal their genetic DNA coding to mix it with their own species of races DNA to help them evolve, whether their agenda's were positive, just for their advancement to ascend to higher dimensions of consciousness and existence, or whether they were negative, were they wanted better genetic's so that they could dominate over other races. That's why humanity has been genetically manipulated by so

many other species of races because
our twelve strands of DNA are
advanced genetics, and when all twelve
strands of DNA are activated we have
the ability to ascend and transcend the
holographically hyperdimensional light
time templar matrix of Creation, and
we can also heal the fabric of the light
filiament structure of the
electromagnetic fields of the Planet.
I learned a lot of this at fifteen years
old by studying the Native American
Indians and other tribal native peoples
around the Planet. I also in my thirties
had the realization that at seven years
old I was taken off Planet onto a ship
morphed of light where a spiritual
being was behind me but I could not
see their face or body, and I was sat in
front of a screen were they were
showng me information of which I
would need later in life, I now believe
they were helping me to go on the
shamanic path so that I could access
my Mer-Ka-Ba field of light, access my
eternal human light body. So these

children that become teenagers are trying to make sense of existence, that's when they become aware of hybrid races and genetic experiments on this Planet and beyond in the Universe. The children with these telepathic connectins to their Star families then start to get heavy downloads in their teenage years because of their questioning of existence, that other normal teenages don't get, unless they have been studying some of these specific subjects, they will have a lessor understanding of these subjects.

So an example of these downloads that a child gets after asking a question to their Star family like a question on God and why we exist, the telepathic response is a paradox like a statement that seems to contradict itself but may nonetheless be true. Or like an answer of a situation or circumstance that exhibits inexplicable or contradictory aspects. Or a statement that is self-contradictory or logically untenable, though based on a valid deduction from acceptable premises. So the telepathic answer from the question a teenager will ask about physics or about God and why do we exist is a paradoxical answer, like we exist because nonexistence could not exist because it would be the denying of existence, and only if existence exists then nonexistence could exist and that's why there is existence. The telepathic downloaded answer about God that a child gets, is like a vision that God is an all that is force and everything that exists are infinite frequency modulations of that same energy that we call God, and that it is fractalized, and the purpose behind God and the Universes existence and fractalizing into infinite aspects of its self, is because God by nature is being everything and nothing at the same time, so God wanted to be someone, and that's why it factualized its self to become someone. And the only number God could divide its self by definition mathematically speaking is infinite which is an abstract number, and because infinity is not a number, rather it exists only as an abstract concept. The concept of fractals and the geometry of the fractals frequencies is the essence of the Universe and the essence of infinity with the mathematical fractals always repeating. So there is a God force that is on a continuum of recreating its self mathematically and infinitely, so that its nonexistence would not be what prevails, which would mean there is nothing.

So many of these children have had interactions with extraterrestrials and are having experiences with their psychic connection to their Star families, that are giving them their downloads of information, and some of these children are having other interactions from more negative races that they have had contact with. Many of these children perceive this intelligence as two divided collectives, and perceive one collective group of races that do not have an agenda, that are all about experience, they are experience based that want expansion for a spiritual expansion, and the other collective group of races that are agenda based, that unfortunately have been controlling and manipulating strongly the evolution and awakening of humanities collective consciousness, and are involved in a lot of negative experiment scenarios like abductions for hybrid programs. From the perspective of these children's experiences, they are experiencing a duality experience of both the negative agenda based races and the spiritual positive experience races.

So what is the agenda based races goal or mission that is denying their existence to humanity and denying and blocking information to humanity, because they also use this information for an agenda that appears to benefit their race, and even more so they are

controlling how information and what type of information gets to peoples subconsciousness, which is the most important part to manipulate a being you influence their subsconcious mind, and then they apply an agenda. So these children are aware of the positive collectives that want expansion of consciousness for humanity, and aware of the negative races that are blocking humanity from knowing the truth about their existence and other races, and the truth of Universal reality and Universal knowledge.
Some of the children say the beings responsible for their positive downloads that have explained the reality of existence are called Anunnaki, but one has to realize that there are many various kinds of Anunnaki, the interaction of the children with the positive ones have been light blue skinned and they have a connection to Celtic people from Planet Gaia, and are specifically connected to one civilization of past history that they

called Hyperborea, they were a mystical people who lived in the north part of the World in the Artic region and its said that they lived to one thousand years old.

In humanities past history through the Greek historian Herodotus he mentioned that just as Plato had cited the Egyptians legend of the sunken island of Atlantis, that there was another Egyptian legend of the continent of Hyperbores in the far north of the Planet. Along with Thule, Hyperborea was one of several terra incognita to the Greeks and Romans, where Pliny, Pindar, and Herodotus, as well as Virgil and Cicero, reported that people lived to the age of one thousand years old and lived a happy fulfilling life in complete happiness. Hecateaus of Abdera also wrote that the Hyperboreans had a circular temple on their island.

The image below is a map of the Arctic by Gerardus Mercator that was first printed in 1595, this image below is the map edition from 1623.

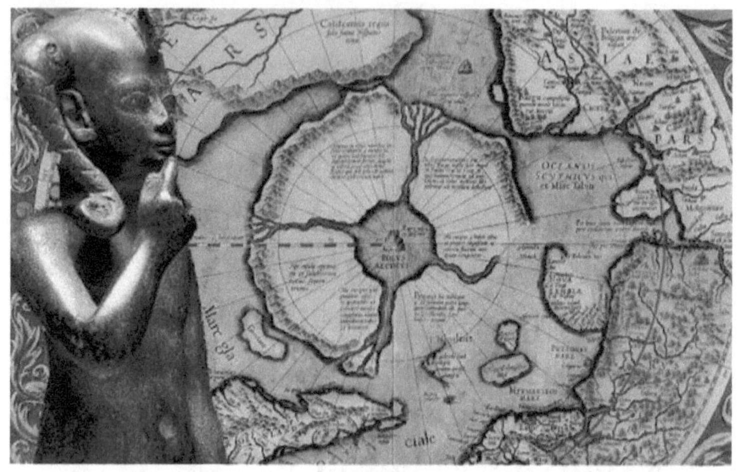

The image below is what the Hyperboreans city looked like.

It was said that the Hyperboreans were giant men that had large beautiful homes adorned with gold, and that their principle occupation was agriculture because they grew grain and had vineyards. John G. Bennett wrote a research paper entitled, The Hyperborean Origin of the Indo-European Culture, in which he claimed the Indo-European homeland was in the far north, which he considered the Hyperborea of classical antiquity. This idea was earlier proposed by Bal Gangadhar Tilak (whom Bennett credits) in his The Artic Home in the Vedas (1903) as well as the Austrian-Hungarian ethnologist Karl Penka (origins of the Aryans, 1883). Also H. P. Blavatsky, Rene Guenon, and Julius Evola, all shared the belief in the Hyperborean polar origins of Mankind and a subsequent solidification and devolution. Hyperborea was the Golden Age polar center of civilization and spirituality, mankind does not rise from the ape, but progressively devolves into the apelike condition as it strays from spirituality and physically from its northen homeland. Robert Charroux first related the Hyperboreans to an ancient astronaut race of reputedly very large, very white people who had chosen the least warm region on the Planet because it corresponded more closely to their own climate on their home Planet.

Bal Gangadhar Tilak was the first popular leader of the Indian Independence Movement. In 1903, he wrote the book The Arctic Home in the Vedas. In it, he argued that the Vedas could only have been composed in the Arctics, and the Aryans brought them south after the onset of the ice age.

So going back to the Anunnaki communicating with the children, they teach the children their back ground and history, but there is also a history in many ancient texts of the Anunnaki on Planet Gaia, but the name Anunnaki is a very general term because it's a species made up of many different races and sub races. Even in between the different races and species of Anunnaki they have many conflicts, because they have many different mixes of genetics with different histories, with different beliefs and are on different paths of experience and evolvution. But there was a group of Anunnaki in texts in human history that were involved with us, that had elongated heads and wore headdresses, it was also said that they used technology wands to communicate directly into human consciousness on the Planet. This Anunnaki group consisted of Enki and Enili two brothers that were know as Gods in ancient Mesopotamia, which was in

Iraq in the middle east, which is in the Sumerians ancient history, they built their first city in the World known as Eridu, which is when they say civilization started. So Enki and Enili were from an extraterrestrial civilization that came from another Star Solar System and put a base on Planet Gaia, and they were involved in the genetic manipulation of already evolving primates to create what we call homosapiens. The texts say that they were genetic engineers on this Planet of different life forms. But I question that because the divine angelic human blood lineages were created over five hundred and eighty million years ago in this Universe, so did they really take human twelve stranded DNA genetics from other Star Solar Systems and then bring them to this Planet and genetically manipulate the angelic human DNA by turning off ten strands, leaving a two stranded DNA activated to enslave this human race into a duality reality to comtrol them use them to build infrastructure and feed off of them, via blood sacrifice cereomonies and feed of humans energetically.

So what would the Annunnaki's agenda be in our time today this is hard to answer because of all the species and sub species of the Anunnaki that have different agenda's. Its clear that some Anunnaki want to dominate and control humanity and genetically manipulate them further, and there are other groups that want to leave humanity with its own freedom to evolve naturally without more genetic manipulations and alterations, that is why there is so much conflict on the Planet today because they are in the back ground behind the scenes. So there are many types of contacts with all these different groups of Anunnaki, some are in dreams, or telepathically in communication only, then you have some abductees saying that they were taken in a beam of light or a beam of light to a craft, some have said a tiny teleport technology ball arrives in their room and they are teleported to the destination off World. Others say that they are the product of Anunnaki genetic manipulation programs that are ongoing on the Planet, which is a creation of hybrids on the Planet, and that the military treats these hybrids as a possible threat to the Planet. These hybrids describe themselves as a product of genetic engineering with added extraterrestrial genetics, and some say they are used in there hybrid breeding programs, and they say these hybrids are a threat to humanity. Many of the woman abductees say they were taken and their genetic were used to create hybrid babies, which many of the women are not happy about and are not ok with the hybrids that have been created. There is also information in these breeding programs about the extraterrestrial race known as the Greys from the Star System Zeti Reticuli taking souls, so imprisoning souls, meaning capturing and enslaving the eternal ultra violet energetic plasma Source consciousness of the being. So it appears the Greys are behind these types of breeding programs, because they proclaim to be a dying race, they say they are near to extinction, and they have claimed to be the human race from the future, this is to convince humanity that we are some how related genetically, so that we have compassion for their species, and get humans to agree on a lower or higher level to give our genetic to them. But I think its possible they are being deceptive and that they want our genetic to up grade their species that could then possibly dominate humanity and even try to take the Planet Gaia for themselves and their hybrid race, they appear to be of negative intentions and knavish with the characteristic of a knave, so dishonest, and fraudlent, with intentions of trickery and deception. Many of these abductee hybrids on the Planet believe this is one of the greatest threats to humanities evolution at the present time, because abductees that have been used by the Greys in these hybrid programs say when they understood what they had been used for and what was going on in these human-grey hybrid programs, and exposed them and their real intentions to the general population on Planet Gaia, they were psychically attacked and that many nearly died, some may have. But these hybrids Star families tell them the Greys physic attacks are directed at the inner technology inside the human soul or inside the eternal ultra violet Source consciousness field of the being, that is called the Mer-Ka-Ba. Which bascically in physics is two vortex fields of energy spinning in different orientations, so opposite directions, and that is what creates a stable human avatar, a stable human vessel, that is viable for the soul to manifest into because the attunement frequency is at the correct vibration for the soul to enter the human vessel and manifest in material form. When this Mer-Ka-Ba field spins in two directions, and is targeted and manipulated by psychic attack or by technology attack, its unbalanced, it then creates illness in the body and rapid disease and even death can be caused by these attacks. This is why most abductees don't speak out publically because they fear the reprocussions of what the Greys will do to them if they reveal anything about their hybrid breeding programs. Some abductees in these Greys programs say their experiences have been astral experiences out of body experiences, where they go to sleep and their souls are projected and pushed out of their bodies, and become conscious that they were on a Grey spacecraft, where they see the Greys and the hybrid babies, and watch the greys experiment on them. These are the Greys that are about four foot tall with big black almond eyes and pointy noses which are extraterrestrials that most abductees say are negative, or which may possibly be programable life forms, that are programmed to carry out specific tasks in some breeding programs, which are different to the Eben Greys that are tall Greys with large noses and are extraterrestrial biological enrtities which have more pear shaped heads. So we have to ask ourselves why are the negative four foot greys so intentionally focused on humanity, well it appears they want to impose their genetics onto Planet Gaia, so that they can be introduced energetically, because its all about frequency and vibration and about DNA genetics, which are programs of frequency patterns, that can vibrate at the highest frequencies of the Universe. Like our twelve stranded DNA that can when fully accessed transend time and space at will, this is why the Greys and other races are abducting and taking our divine angelic human linerages of genetic DNA genepools and mixing it with their own species, so they can have rapid evolution allowing them to

access a Mer-Ka-Ba field to be able to
transcend time and space and access
the eternal realms outside of this
holographical hyperdimensional light
time templar matrix. Now that's the
truth of true reality and why all these
different species of extraterrestrial
races are coming and taking our
genetic material without our consent
and some with consent from higher
level agreements for experience and
growth as spiritual beings. So its all
about the DNA genetics, the higher the
amount of strands in the DNA the
more advance beings are created with
extremely powerful abilities that can
become manifested as eternal beings.
So its about the DNA physics the
science of matter and its energy fields
that can vibrated at higher frequencies.
Because if a being or species can
control the frequency patterns of the
program within the DNA structure of
one species of that collective schematic
blueprint, then they can insert
themselves onto another species and

manipulate them and their projected course of evolution. The positive human military from Planet Gaia have been helping some of the abductees get away from these negative agenda based Greys and their genetic programs, even saving some of their lifes. The human military have also put implants into the brains or heads of the abductees so that they can communicate with them directly. Some of the abductees contact with the human military groups normally starts when the abductees recover their past memories of experiences in the SSP, the secret space programs in this life time or from past incarnations. Where some abductees were in many different SSP programs working with many different extraterrestrial races in many different Galaxies, a few where in the military in the SSP working in the group known as the Dark Fleet, which was formed by the Nazi's, and the German SSP. And there are also many factions within all the SSP which have separated and are no longer working on the same agenda or mission. The abductees say the human military helped them recover their memories and protected them from the negative Grey extraterrestrials, and it appears that the Greys are hijacking and collecting souls, which does not seem to be a positive agenda at all.

Many of these SSP groups from multiple nations and secret societies like the German Vril society amongst many others have spit away from their original groups, and have created other groups and factions, as have many different exterterrestrial races and their groups. This is because some groups realized the intentions of others in their original group organizations were to take humanity towards a negative timeline, that benefited the negative human and extraterrestrial groups agendas, to push humanity away from the positive timeline of evolution towards ascension into a fifth dimensional state of consciousness and experience, this is because then humanity cannot be dominated, controlled, and enslaved by other races.

To understand this splitting of all the different groups between humans and extraterrestrials and their different groups and factions, you have to go back to the time frame in the nineteen thirties leading up to World war two and the original planned intentional agenda of Adolf Hitler, who spoke about having contact with and was working with extraterrestrials from the Aldebaran Star System, who were blue eyed with blonde hair. Adolf Hitlers original supposed plan was to ally, and treaty with the Aldebaran race to make it possible for the Aldebaran race to aid and assist him during the coming war to take over the World, and work together to remove the Draconian Reptilians presence from the Planet. The problem with Adolf Hitlers plan was that the Draconian Reptilian empire had learned information of the plan and knew about the Aldebaran races agenda to help Hitler remove their presence from the Planet, so the Draconian Reptilians psychically influenced the humans from the higher dimension to stop this united plan via mind control, this was when the Nazi faction known as the Dark Fleet aligned with the reptilians. This manipulated psychic influence behind the scenes in the astral realm is why the Nazi's became negative and brutal towards others with their genocidal agenda, so it was the reptilians psychic mind control that took Hitler and the Nazi's off there original planned mission towards a positive timeline with no Draconian influence on the Planet. The Aldebaran race also psychically became aware that if they stayed on the Planet to work with Hitler at that time that they would also be mind controlled and influenced by the extremely powerful psychic Draconian reptilians, so they left going back to the Aldebaran Star System.

But they have come back at this time to the Planet in our timeline to help in the evolutionary process of humanities ascension into the fifth dimension of consciousness. They are aligned with the positive split away group from the Nazi's original SSP, and many positive races are working with many positive human SSP groups, and other break away civilization societies from other nations. Some of these groups are in Antartica, others are in Inner Earth, others are living in floating cities, or off Planet in huge spacecraft, some are staying in other parts of the Solar System. But the intention of all of these Christos consciousness Collectives of all these positive races and groups, is a unified agenda for the human race to achieve the ascension process into the fifth dimension of consciousness.

So what are the current agendas today and objectives of the Draconian Reptilian empire and the negative Anunnaki in their endeavors with humanity and the Planet. It appears they are creating hybrid super soldiers mentally, physically, and psychically in their endeavour to try to take over the Planet and humanity. So why do the reptilians want the Planet Gaia, well its because they are a species of beings that are from different densities of consciousness, and because they have accessed a higher density of consciousness it means they are able to connect better with their higher selfs, this means they have had more intergration with their higher mind, which allows them to have much more multidimensional depth and connection to the structure of existence of the hyperdimensional light time templar matrix of the holographical Creation, which makes them extremely powerful psychic beings. This also does not necessarily mean that because they have accessed a higher state of consciousness, that they are positive or have positive intended agendas, because to become truly positive with your intention of manifestation its really about developing the heart space, which is about soul development. Also the reptilians are great in size and numbers and they are very intelligent, so they are above humanity on the food chain and so they feed of humanity literally and energetically, because we are extremely powerful energetic beings of light. And the current agendas today and objectives of the Aldebaran race and other allies in their endeavors with humanity and the Planet, is to make sure there is not a take over by the negative groups and that humanity ascends to the fifth dimension.

So what is really going on with all these different extraterrestrial races and the hybrid genetic programs like the Greys and other genetic hybrid programs by other species of races, and why the conflict between these species to conquer and claim Planet Gaia as their territory. This is because many of these species have genetic connections to humanity, because they were all apart of giving their DNA gene pools to the great experiment to create our species of human beings. Also this is a repeating cycle that has been going on for millenia in this Planets ancient past and throughout humanities history. So we are intimately connected genetically to and through the many different DNA gene pools of many extraterrestrial species, because of different races taking part and agreeing to give their genetics in the great Universal genetic experiment agreement to create the human race. So these races perceive this an an open door of opportunity to upgrade and bolster their genetic gene pools, via hybrid programs, genetic frequency manipulation, and via consciousness development and control. Then when they have upgraded themselves genetically they will be more powerful beings than humanity, because with our fully activated twelve strands of DNA, the human divine schematic blueprint genetics can travel at the speed of light, and teleport multidimensionally, and can step inside and outside of space and time, allowing us to access the eternal reams outside of this holographical hyperdimensional light time templar matrix of Creation. So that means with our mixed genetics the negative species of races could take over control of Planet Gaia and then they could control the course of evolution on the Planet, but the Yanas Ascended Masters, the Founder races, and the Christos Collectives will not allow this to happen. And the truth is that the Christos Collectives have already won this great spiritual battle in the higher dimensions of the celestial ether realms, we now just have to win the spiritual battle in this lower dimensional realm.

Then we come to the other races of the blue eyed and blonde haired six to seven feet tall Nordics, and the eight foot tall Tall chalky skinned Whites, which are two completely different orders, who have been working with the Worlds militaries, and the Aldebaran race are the blue eyed and blonde haired beings that also describe the Nordic races features, but they have no relation genetically or other wise with the negative Greys, and so these Aldebaran are the ones that are aligned in cooperation with humanities positive militaries to aid and guide humanity towards a positive timeline. But these positive races helping do not appear to be dominate in their direction of help, this is because they are not gender based and therefore appear much more passive in there approach rather than an active approach. This is because they are not permitted within their own society through their belief system to interact with humanity on the type of lower level we would expect, this is because it would step over the line and cross the line of Universal law, that states that other species should not interact with other races evolutionary course of development, because it would take away the opportunity and ability to grow and raise their consciousness to evolve spiritually. But on the flip side we have the Reptilians, the negative Anunnaki, the Greys, and other negative races interacting with humanity, and taking our genetics and creating hybrid species, and even hijacking souls, which appears to me to be enslaving eternal ultra violet plasma Source consciousness souls individually. So they are negatively affecting humanities evolution, which is contradictory to and against Universal law of non intervention of other species, and it actually appears although it does not apply to these negative species, or simply they just ignore the Universal laws of non intervention with other species evolving. Because they have been genetically manipulating humanity, hiding the truth and ancient knowledge of who we are genetically and suppressing conscious evolution, and the knowledge of humanities genetics

to access our eternal human light body
so that we can evolve and transcend
our way of being, and they have even
derailed it directly, and even been
intentionally poisoning our body's with
deadly chemicals, and poisoning our
minds via mind control techniques
especially in the human subliminal
subconscious mind, and have mass
murdered humanities vast cultures on
a continuum for at least thirteen
thousand years via human blood
sacrifice, wars, and via toxic chemicals,
just like the biological weapons of war
known as vaccines, which are really
about damaging the human genetics,
and along with the deadly radiation
damaging military grade frequency
microwave weapons systems like 5G,
which is mass genocide and total
democide. Most would perceive this as
an absolute contradiction of Universal
law because we perceive the aggressive
manipulative interfering negative races
are effecting evolution of humanity,
and perceiving the positive races as to

passive or not helping humanity enough, is because this all relates and ties into metaphysical denomics in relation and terms of consciousness, because there is the higher self in what we call the fifth dimension, which is a higher frequency band width were we are all extremely highly conscious, which goes beyond the physical mind and three dimensional conscious minds understanding of ones self or higher self. But that higher fifth dimensional self is aware of all the co-creations that they are involved with and interacting with in this lower dimension in this incarnation on the Planet in this physical plane of existence, and the higher self is the one who is making soul contracts and agreements with other races and different kinds of beings, whether they are negative or positive. The reason our higher selfs are agreeing and making these soul contracts is because there is an exchange of energy, that the higher mind of self, the soul, benefits from this exchange of energy, because there is a learning lesson which occurs that we can take as an opportunity to take those aspects of our consciousness to be able to get intergrated within our DNA to be able to heal and this allows the soul to become much more evolved. Also if this soul learning experience of different types of evolution in different species and interaction with other species did not occur then there would be no point of experience in the physical realities of Creation. We all have contracts with other Star races, these contracts are agreements of expression of ones soul in the physical realms of the holographical hyperdimensional light time templar matrix. So there is an agreement from the higher fifth dimensional self that there will be an interaction, so an exchange of energy of information. So sometimes it is a positive experience, and some times it is a negative experience, this a polarised experience which is a different exchange of information and energy, and in this duality dimension of reality this by design to be polarized this way for a different type of both experiences of positive and negative. The value of the negative is experience and for the opportunity of expansion of spiritual growth.

So when we try to perceive the future, we have to understand that the Planet has an electromagnetic field that is the aura field that is the energetic etheric body of the consciousness matrix of the Planet, this electromagnetic field of the planet contains and emits quantum waves of probabilities, some of these quantum waves are stronger than others, that are higher probabilities of future possible timelines of manifestation in terms of physics into the physical matrix. This is why some people on the Planet can read or see into the future, because they are resonating at the frequency of these quantum waves from the Planets electromagnetic field, and so they have

the ability to read the quantum waves
of future possibilities allowing them to
make future predictions. So these
people actually reading physics, not
factual future events that are going to
manifest and happen, they are only
reading predicted future possibilities of
possible future manifested timelines,
because they are not determined
probabilities, because none of these
timelines are definate fixed
probabilities of manifested timelines
yet. So many on the Planet have
perceived humanity may have an huge
depopulation timeline event, but you
have to perceive this from another
perspective, because the Planet has her
own electromagnetic field of
consciousness which is connected and
interlinked to all the individual
consciousness of the beings living in
her ecosystems, living on her celestrial
body, and the Planet has consciously
decided to evolve and move her
consciousness to the higher fifth
dimension density of existence,

therefore we humans have to evolve our individual consciousness to the fifth dimensional reality of existence to be able to stay living in the physical realm on this Planet. Or if we stay in the third dimension of consciousness we have to die and incarnated on another three dimensional Planet, because you cannot stay on the Planet because your body will not be able to handle the higher fifth dimensional frequency. You also have to understand any negative interactions that people are experiencing on the Planet are just a part of the process of evolving to the higher mind, to the higher level of consciousness. Because with consciousness there is only consciousness and what is not conscious is disintergrated and also known as darkness which are the negative narratives of lower dimensional conflicts and negative interactions, but that part is also consciousness to, but it is unconscious because it is not intergrated into balance, into a state of harmony with the self or higher self. So once the unconscious aspect of our collective of all souls on the Planet has intergrated and aligned with with the Source field or zero point field of Creation creating harmonious balance, then we can make the quanum shift and jump into the higher fifth density of consciousness, and so this is just a part of the process of evolution of a species and a Planet to higher densities of existence.

So to understand why the matrix's design of lived experience in the negative dark polarity exists, and why the Ying and Yang effect of experience is occuring, and why the higher light frequencies of experience is not in total control of the Universe, and why all species are not harmonious and living in bliss all loving and caring for one another living in peace. Well it is because of polarity, and polarity is not a division of one element, but instead polarity is the disintergration of that unifed element in the first place. So really they create each other, so that the one entity, lets say one being of self, an individual soul or a collective of a species can make sense, because without one aspect of it, it can be in the masculine or negative polarity or in the left side of the logical brains perspective, because then the other polarity would not make sense. So to understand this if we look at the Universe and perceive its structure, and there was only the structure without meaning, without content or context then the structure would not even make any sense, would not exist. Because what creates that structure, what is creating, if no creating then there would be nothing, so it would not exist itself. But if there is creative meaning added to that structure then the structure makes sense, and then is a structure of something, something of meaning, a perspective of meaning of a specific type of meaning to the individual self or the collective of a species. Because if a meaning has no structure it cannot make sense, so therefore it cannot exist. So this means duality polarity needs to exist in order for the individual entities that we know as the actual Universe, as consciousness itself to even exist.

Now lets discuss the reality of different frequencies of dimensions, which are different physical planes of existence, they are a place not a location, but rather they are a physical place of space of spectrums of existence in space and time, in which the frequency and vibration is fixed to a determined tune, because it has its own signature frequency. So when people perceive that we are going to enter the fifth dimension, many are misunderstanding the actual metaphysical concept of what this means. Because what we are actually doing is transitioning towards the fourth density of consciousness, because density is about the state of being, about the evolution of ones self awareness of one evolution of

Consciousness. So the difference between densities is the resonance of frequency creating different ways of being, meaning different states of perceptions of lived experience, and different ways to perceive the meaning of existence.

So if we can comprehend the different frequencies of different dimensions, and that if a third dimensional being went into the fifth dimension, because they are operating at the lower frequency, they may not be able to interact with that fifth density matter because it is resonating at a higher frequency in that fifth dimension realm. This is because we are multidimensional beings and our physical human avatar body's have many facets that are fractural in nature, these fractual facets are all operating and vibrating at different frequency levels, multidimensional levels of existence, all facets of our multidimensional being exists at the same time, interconnected.

Now going back to when there are interactions with other beings, other races relating to material physical abductions, there are many different types of abductions, like face to face physical encounters, but there are also abductions and to explain this we have to discuss the schematic blueprint of our physical consciousness, that first exists as a whole graphic element, that then gets abducted, so this way the information exchanged gets directed at the physical consciousness without necessarly having to take or abduct any materialized crystalized form of the physical consciousness itself, or physical material body.

So what are the other dimensional existences and why do many types of beings interact with many different people on the Planet, and download data or visions of other dimensions like the fifth dimension. Well you have to realize that in this context to many citizens of humanity it is one of the greatest mysteries of all of humanity and the Planet Gaia's history. So who are the highest beings of ancient texts, who were the great avatars like Lord Shiva, Lord Ganesha, Lord Krishna, Buddha, Christ, and others from other societies, who were they really, and how do they fit into it all, because we are living in a Universe that is polarised between negative and positive, between black and white, and Ying and Yang, which is actually a symbol of the metaphor for this Universe. So who are these higher density beings and deities, well really they are a representations of archetype aspects of consciousness, and archetype structures are structures of meaning, which is an aspect of our consciousness, and consciousness has its own schematic blueprint mapping structure of different aspects of its self, like it is represented in our chakra energy system, and an archetypal energy represents an idea of a possibility, that is combined in itself in layers of idea's, which is in fractal system. So this is why Deities exist and why people have interacted with them. Well these deities of well known ancient avatars are actually representations of not just one archetypal energy, they represent many kinds of achetypes and consciousness that are behind the Co-Creation of the incarnation of life, of the channeling of information and sharing of information that they are giving to collective consciousnesses in service of life itself. So when these deities have shown up in certain past time frames in our history, it was because the whole of humanity's higher fifth dimensional aspect of consciousness as a collective agreed to manifest them into that time to share knowledge for the whole human races consciousness collective to benefit with enlightenment.

So if we can perceive that there are many different extraterrestrial species of races and all have their many sub species of hybrid races, its then hard to generalize one race or another, because

they are all interconnected genetically
and karmically, just as we are
connected with them, because we have
a possible twenty two different genetics
from other extraterrestrail races in our
genetic make up, that is the make up of
our divine angelic human schematic
blueprint template, of our eternal
avatar temple design. So if we perceive
this connection and interaction
between all species of races on many
levels on a karmic level, we perceive
that there are many karmic cycles of
energy and evolution, of all the
different races that are apart of our
genetic make up, are all karmically
playing out their different manifested
roles in physical experience all at once,
all karmically interlinked in the same
present moment. This is why all the
different races have great interest in
what happens in humanities evolution,
because we have their DNA, their
genetic gene pools of information, so
we are connected to their collective
consciousness, so that means what ever

happens to humanity effects them and influences their own collective consciousnesses evolution directly, via the interconnected karmic cycles. It appears by design of the holographical hyperdimensional light time templar matrix, all beings and races are shown in one form or another that their individual goal is to ascend to a higher dimension of existence to evolve, this is the case generally, all species of consciousness are shown that there is a constant in the Universe that is called evolution. This is the constant heart beat or rhythum of the Creation, of the Universe that is not directed by will or action it's the constant beat of evolution via the Generative Principle of Creation, which is the heart beat of Creation. So you can either expand your consciousness for positive evolution or suppress it for a negative devolution experience. But the philosophy behind it is that there is no such thing as deevolution because if you moved in the direction of darkness towards the negative experience, the Ascended Masters would say that is an opportunity to grow spiritually and expand your consciousness, because you would get to know more aspects of your consciousness that were not in balance or alignment previously, and because of the negative experience you can then grow and expand. So what are the differences of eternal lives to short life spans, this is because our divine angelic human blueprint genetics are eternal, but humanity has been genetically manipulated by many species, and then the Anunnaki decided to then manipulate ten out of our twelve strands of DNA to be deactivated, which has lead to short life spans, and an imprisionment of lower consciousness in the duality mindset, which most of humanity has been operating via there subconscious uncontrolled minds. So it appears the Anunnaki have genetically manipulated humanity to stop us becoming an eternal race, when we were on the fringe of doing so around thirteen thousand years ago, and to use us as slaves, and so humans could be harvested for their eternal Source high energy as a resource. But others may see it from a deeper perspective that its related to the idea that how there is the different multidimensional aspects of the soul, which is interconnected and involves the mind the psyche, the subconscious, the emotional body, the physical body, the astral spiritual body, and these different body's expand in cycles of energy, which is directly connected to astrological patterns, so this is the process of how we get to develop all those body's, to eventually unite all body's into one unifed light field, which is known as the Merkaba field, the eternal human light body field of immortality. So we have to teach ourselves to be able to connect to the esoteric force, to the zero point electromagnetic energy field of Creation to expand your light field and self heal to transmute our DNA, then that extends your life span, until you can connect all light fields into one harmonious light field, that is also known as the eternal human rainbow body of light.

Many of these other races that have life spans of hundreds of years, many have around a thousand to eight hundred years, but many choose to leave their physical biological avatar body before the end of their full life spans by several hundred years, this is to do with cycles, to do with patterns of energy and time frames, because every year there is a cycle of evolutionary transformation of expansion. So these cycles are about the inner soul cycles of expansion and evolutionary development, and so depending on the idea of the manifested life time when it was structured by their original conception of space and time, the consciousness collective of that race may have put in place a predetermined time frame to leave the material biological body earlier than the full life span expectancy of the biological avatar that they manifested into. This is because they recognize that they only need to achieve a certain amount of yearly evolutionary cycles of energy, to conduct their missions and agendas in that manifested physical avatar, and when a race evolves to understand the energies that create and sustain life, and the soul cycles, why would you stay in that physical material avatar body if it has reached a point of old age and is declining in its function. So they leave the avatar before this occurs, because they know were they are going after they leave the biological avatar.

So we humans also have the ability to extend our life spans by the correct strict high vibrational diet, and with key disciplined practices like mind disciplines of meditation, and with core chi energy practices, which raises our body frequency allowing us to connect to the frequencies of the electromagnetic fields of the Planet and the zero point energy field of the

Creation, which allow us to extend our life spans longer, until you can access your fully activated immortal light body to ascend and transcend the matrix, and access the eternal realms.

So we have to have a reintergration of our higher minds by raising our consciousness frequency, but this is different for every soul depending on what they chose before incarnation from a higher level of mind, and it depends also on your individual ability to decipher information on this Planet to the use that collected data to advance your own personal evolution, via your intentinal manifestion of this evolutionary change from within.
So what are the incarnation cycles about and why do we choose to have them at specific times, this is because your spirit, your soul has chosen to move its perspective, which is your view point of experience, and move into a parallel incarnation of its own material physical matrix of manifested physical experience, so that means this

is not linear because everything is happening at the same time in the present moment of now. So we move into other incarnations for experience and evolutionary spiritual growth.

So what we come to learn about incarnation cycles of souls is that it is the machinery of this Universe, and so the purpose of this Universe is to get to know ourselves from a general perspective from many different points of view infinitly, because time is an illusion and so it never ceases to exist, in these constructs that we are creating because the Universe never ceases to exist, so we are in a constant state of expansion of our consciousness. This is because we are eternal Source light beings, we are goddesses and gods, we are angels, manifesting in lower dimensions to grow spiritually by evolving to reconnect to our higher vibrational god brains, because we are the eternal Source fields infinite perspective of itself, so that the Source field knows itself, or put this way, so

that god knows itself from infinite points of view.
So we are responsible for our own incarnations and lives and of our creations of our own encompassing realities, so we have the power and rights to change an incarnational contract that we have previously agreed upon in the higher dimensions with other races, and if you evolve to understand the bigger picture, then you can manifest to no longer agree with the previous soul contract that you made and agreed upon. So you can change and break the original soul contract because you are an eternal interdimensional light being that is sovereign, meaning you are one that exercises supreme permanent authority of self, and you are free to choose this because you are a Source being from the Source collective unifed field. You need to understand that you are an energetic plasma Source being weighing twenty one grams from the Source collective and that no other

individual Source being from the Source field collective has power over you, or the right to dominate or interfere in your evolution, especially when you expand your consciousness awareness field and become aware of interference, whether it is a soul contract agreement or other wise, you can manifest a change or desolvement of the original agreement at any point of time, once you have become consciously aware of what is taking place, this is because you are a divine Source Creator and this is your divine sovereign right via Universal and Cosmic law, and this is also because the power of Creation lies in the the present moment of now.

Also you come to be aware that the above is below and the below is above which is a well known fact in metaphysical laws of this Universe, so when we desire a transition we can say no to previous agreed soul contracts, so that we can change direction or the orientation of our manifestations into the enveloping physical reality in which we reside. So because above is the same as below in regards to our lower selfs consciousness that is linked in connection to our higher selfs consciousness, there is no separation because information can flow down to us from the higher mind, but also information can be sent from the lower mind up to the higher mind to effect a change of physical manifestation and direction to move towards, even breaking soul contracts that no longer serve us. So we can from the lower dimension of consciousness change the direction we are going in, and choose to manifest a different direction of manifested experience that will allow us to evolve into a new physical matter experience that are no longer bound by previous soul agreement contracts. This is also because there is no separation from the higher fifth and lower third consciousness states of mind, so there is only a desintergration of perception, because there is no separation, because we are always collaborating with the connected lower and higher mind on the multidimensional dynamic level of relating energy that's always in motion, in the motion of manifesting experience for spiritual growth and evolution. So for humanity to evolve freely they need to understand the hidden knowledge and wisdom of the souls incarnation evolutionary process and understand energy and its different vibrational frequencies and its cycle patterns. It is also known that when we look back at human evolutionary history the hidden factual truth is that at around Atlantis times humans on this Planet were in the last stages of the evolution process of becoming super advanced human beings, via accessing higher frequencies of consciousness to activate all of our twelve strands of DNA, that would of activated our eternal Merkaba human light body, which means humanity was about to become free and eternally sovereign from the interference of other species of races, but that was stopped by genetic manipulation by the negative Anunnaki group. They did this via the karmic cycles of patterns that are contained within our divine angelic human DNA schematic blueprint, they did this via negative intention to make our schematic blueprint unstable to cause humanities collective to manifest a physical catastrophe in the physical matrix to try to wipe out the entire advanced human race. But this caused humanity to fractualize and separate and go in different directions, some survived and went into the Inner Earth, others moved to Antarctica, so these separated human societies are our ancestors that did not split into different directions, and that's why they still contain the ancient knowledge and wisdom because they never lost it, they are the ones that have always helped humanity by sharing ancient knowledge and wisdom, and they are the ones from the Inner Earth that have been communicating psychically with the human surface population to aid in our evolution back to our original higher states of consciousness. So the negative intention of the despicable Anunnaki was the purpose of control and domination of the human surface population after being split in different directions via the catastrophe and a continuum of conflicts, which are constantly created to keep us in a low vibrational duality reality of consciousness to stop us remembering who we truly are, and to deny us attainment of the original information we had within our DNA genetic gene pools to deny humanity and stop humanities evolution. So that the negative Anunnaki and their negative Draconian reptilian allies and their negative Grey allies can dominate, manipulate and control humanies evolution, while also stealing our DNA genetic information to create hybrid races to advance their own species with our super advanced genetics that can transcend time and space beyond the hyperdimensional matrix of Creation, allowing them a massive leap into evolutionary development. This is the true agenda behind these fallen races like the Anunnaki and their ally races, who are service to self beings.

So in the fragmented times of today on the Planet with the deception and manipulation of information, it is down to the individual soul to attain and decipher this ancient knowledge and wisdom of information to help in our own individual evolutionary process, which in turn that will help the consciousness collective of humanity evolve into the higher dimensions and access our divine Source Sovereign rights to access our super human divine schematic blueprint to evolve to an eternal human race.

Also supposedly near the beginning of every 26000 year ascension cycle the higher dimensional beings of light, and the Mother ray vortex, will banish and imprison the Draco reptilians, Greys, Anunnaki, and other negative ETs to the Eridanus Super Void, which may be percieved as at the very edge of our Universe. By transiting the negative ETs to this far region of space, this practically evicts them to exist within a Void as in a form of an enclosed sphere, quarantining them from the rest of the Universe, this is so that no harm will then ever come to the organic inhabitants of our Universe. Also this Void is practically isolated from the Neural Network of Source and lies outside the open loop fountain of free energetics. So they are left to their chosen fate, no longer able to siphon and prey upon the energetics of other innocent entities, left to exist within a closed energetic circuit for the rest of their lifes, until total self energetic consumption occurs, when they run out of chi energy and die, leaving the physical plane returning back to the Source field.

CHAPTER TWELVE

Final Analysed Axiomatic Apparent Conclusions

The Knowledge, of truth, freedom and love, is the work of awakening the masses to the true nature of the Ego Mind, to create an an environment to encourage all Worldwide citizens to use their critical thinking Mind, and to have courage to face their own Inner dark shade of Self the negative of our Selves, and to practice the Natural Law of positive Expressions, understanding that what we use to create that of expressions of Generative Polarity, in the positive it is Consciousness from Love, and in the negative it is Unconsciousness from Fear, then in the expression of Initiating expressions of how it starts, in the positive it is

acceptance of Truth of Knowledge, and in the negative it is Ignorance and the refusal of Truth, then in the expression of Internal expression of whats happening inside us, in the positive it is Internal monarchy of Sovereignty, and in the negative it is Internal Anarchy causing Confusion, then in the expression of whats happening in our environment in our Society, in the positive its Freedom of External Anarchy, and in the negative it is Control of External Monarchy, then in the expression of Manifestation the result we create, in the positive it is Order and all manifested is Good, and in the negative it is Chaos which manifests Evil.

The truth is that the Law of Freedom is known, that freedom and morality are directly proportional, and as morality increases, so does freedom increase. And as morality declines, so does freedom decrease. So if humanity instead practices Love, coming from their Heart-Mind with Love in their manifestations, then humanity will then experience and know, and be in a state of Freedom, by accessing higher levels of vibrational Consciousness. The problems is the masses of which many are unaware that they are in a Mindset of Defacto Satanism, which will lead them down the path of absolute domination with complete enslavement. This is why we must share our ancient knowledge with others of the Mind, of the Ego, of Source, of Universal history of the Angelic Seed Wars, of DNA Biotechnology, of Spirit, of Nature, of Energy, of the Eternal, of Consciousness, of Physics and Psychology of the Mechanics and Mechanisms of Life and the Creation. Then we can evolve Individually and Collectively as planned by our Creators from Source the Yanas Ascended Masters, that designed us to evolve into Embodied Eternal Angelic Human Light beings, to evolve as a Collective Human Eternal race to take control of our destiny as a species. We must pass knowledge to all Worldwide citizens about their Schematic Blueprint within their DNA, that informs the Luminous Energy Field the Software to upgrade and then manifest and grow a new body via the Hardware the DNA, to grow a new Eternal Human Light Body, but to attain this one must overcome the negative polarity of our individual Ego's.

Namaste I recognize the Eternal Immortal Soul within each of you, the human Spirit, the Divine spark within, we are beings of peace of light and love and Pro-Life. Namaste to all.

So the other Conclusion we come to realize is that the Super Advanced living DNA Holographical Conscious Projection is the structure of reality, and constructed by thought forms, that materialize physical manifested Geometric Matter in a Holographical fashion. It is created with distinctive

Scalar Energy structures that are unique and tangible, they are Dimensional fields that are slightly oval in shape, that nest within themselves in layers. The Intrinsic Eternal Spirit of the Oneness Collective Consciousness is that which brings fourth Source Intellectual Intelligence, known as Yunasai.

We come to realize that the multidimensional Holographical Creation is constructed of Space, Time and Matter which creates our realities, and is objective with embodiment, and being embodied in Animation via Sacred Geometric form of vibrating Light at different frequencies, creating different Densities that are layered with Fifteen Dimensional Light Time Matrix's, that create this Holographical Universe and the whole Hyper-Dimensional Light Matrix of living Conscious Spirit. This is the construct of the Original Matrix Template that we currently are manifested into in Animated form, inside Time and Space in this Holographical Super Advanced DNA Biotechnology. We also learn that we will evolve via our Consciousness by activating our DNA to Ascend and then Transcend back into the realm of Source.

We come to understand that Spirit is in all things for it is Eternal Source Energy that's forever existing, its just materializing and dematerializing in different forms of manifestation, and it exists outside the confines of Time and Space in the Eternal Spirit realms, beyond the Holographical Light Creation.

We also can come to the Conclusion that we are the Yanas Ascended Masters acting out Character roles in a Holographical Living Animated Movie, that we come to participate in, in the physical Animated experience of Life, and to learn about Ourselves, to gain more Knowledge and Insight and to grow Spiritually. We also realize that the Yanas Ascended Masters

Consciousness had an Original Covenant when they defined the precise rules of the Holographical Animated Movie, a Light Time Matrix, with a Love based system that was created with Free Will.

So the Creations Consciousness is the Core substance of the building blocks of the materialized Cosmos and all Life. So our thoughts are attributes of Consciousness, and so our thoughts permeate through in which Consciousness manifests it's self into the materialized Living DNA Sacred Geometric Matter Hologram.

So solid form is a construct of an illusion in the Mind, and is perceived and determined by the Dimensional relationship between the Consiousness observing a Holographical object of Light and the Consciousness of which the object is made up of. We come to understand that our Consciousness of our Human thinking Mind resides in the Fourth Dimension, and that we perceive our animated Avatar in the

Third Dimension below, so we learn when manifesting into physical Animated form our Consciousness always resides One Dimension above. So the perception of reality of solidity and externalization is defined by the osilating rates between Dimensionalized units of materialized objects of Consciousness. So it's the Consciousness of the Observers Dimensional frequency that is the difference between a manifested Animated structure and a thought. So thought projection is manifesting Animated reality that's built soild and externalized by the relationships between the frequencies of our Chi Core focused Attention and those of the projected thought forms, that we perceive as our physical realities, that are the thought forms of the races mass Collective Consciousness that resides One Dimension below in the lower frequency band of the Third Dimension, while our Consciousness is operating One band higher in the

Fourth Dimension. So thought fields create reality and are energetic field units of Conscious Awareness that directly effect materialized animated reality, and so this means that they are One and the Same, with the Intrinsic essence of Spirit.

We come to understand that the Animated Holographical Creation of manifested living DNA realities is a complex system of interwoven fabricated energy field constructs, that are all constructed upon Dimensionalized sets of Scaler grids, and that the Dimensions are arranged into sets of Fifteen, and that they form the Blueprint for a Fifteen Dimensional system called a Light Time Matrix. You then come to understand that a Dimension is one particular single rhythm band of Scalar frequency and that there are Fifteen distinctive contrasting Scalar frequency bands within our Light Time Matrix.

These Fifteen Dimensions are then grouped into sets of Three Dimensions individually, which also then create Five separate reality fields that are called Density Universes, with each of the Five Density Universes representing a particular level of matter and biology that's exclusive and definitive to its Intrinsic frequency rates of current that are changing direction every second, and are measured in Herz.

So we also come to perceive that all of the Sacred Geometric Animated living Spirit beings of our Light Time Matrix exist within One of the Five Density Universes.

The First Density is of Matter constructed of Carbon and consists of Dimensions One, Two and Three, where Animated Carbon based incarnated life form species of races reside, in the Physical Matter Density of molecules that are the fabric of the Life Field on Planet Gaia our Mother Earth, and it is also the same on other

Planetary Star Systems residing in Density One.

The Second Density is of Etheric Carbon Matter that consists of Dimensions Four, Five and Six, where Carbon Silica Matter Soul races reside with an Avatar of Fifty percent Silica combined with Fifty percent Carbon. This changes there Avatar structure into Fifty percent Silica Quartz Crystals, which is what happens as you raise your frequency and rise in Density, as the biological Avatar becomes more Silica based to access the higher Dimensional frequencies of Consciousness.

The Third Density is of Etheric Matter and consists of Dimensions Seven, Eight and Nine, where there is an Etheric Matter biology that has no Carbon, so these beings become Crystalline beings of formed Matter, these are the Higher Soul races manifesting in this structured form. There manifested forms and reality fields are living Crystalline Matrices,

and there are also beings that look like crystalline transparent Light beings, and that's what we evolve into Etheric Matter beings of Light.
The Fourth Density is of Hyroplasmic Pre Matter that consists of Dimensions Ten, Eleven and Twelve, where there is Crystalline Liquid Light Pre Matter biology. These are the advanced Avatar races of Christos Consciousness at the level of Crystalline Liquid Light, they are also known as Hydroplasm beings that are Highly Spiritually Advanced.
The Fifth Density is of Anti Matter and consists of Dimensions Thirteen, Fourteen and Fifteen, where they have a Standing Wave Pattern Flame Avatar of Anti Matter biology. These are the Rishis races with fully expanded Sun Bodies, they are also known as the Sphere Light beings.

Activating the Chakra Energy System to Awaken our Kundalini Life Force Energy to Activate our Pineal Gland our Third Eye

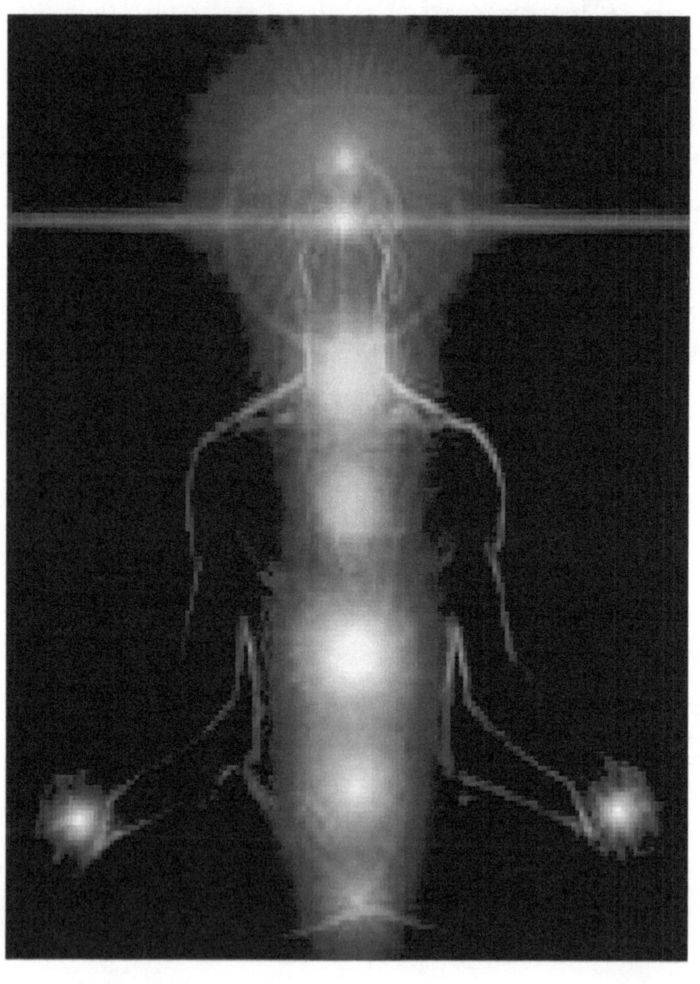

Closing Culmination
Of Conclusions

I hope this information can help in your understanding of the history of the Universe, and the Creation that is the Super Advanced Holographical DNA Biotechnology, and that of the mechanical sciences that it is formed from into animated existence. And I hope this also gives an understanding of the races that created the Primal Sound Waves of Conscious Matter with the Intrinsic essence of Eternal Spirit. I hope this information will also help you to understand our current manifested present Planetary Human drama, while also relating to the Intergalactic multidimensional Cosmic Spiritual Seed War of Christos Consciousness.

To achieve the Merkaba Diamond Sun Light Body Activation and Ascension, the disciplines we must undertake and practice are Meditation, Energy practices, Light work practices, Sacred Ceremonies, and to achieve Clarity through Silence through Breath work is important. But one of the main keys to higher vibrational frequencies of our Human Avatars is Diet, with the right high vibrational foods that we need to ingest to heal and access our dormant DNA strands to activate our Eternal Rainbow Diamond Sun Light Bodies.

I wish you all Eternal Blessings on your path to Ascension and to Transcending the Hyper-Dimensional Matrix of the Creation. Namaste Love Life Lee.

Weilding our Eternal Chi
Life Force Energy

Using Energetic Magic Words & Symbols To Raise Your Consciousness & Change Your Envoloping Reality

The word magic is the art of using sacred sounds and symbols, and hidden forces to direct and control energy to produce certain desired effects or marvels. All words have magicial properties, however certain words have more magicial properties for the reason that they carry more energy and intention. This is why during magic rituals certain words are used more than others, because word magic uses sacred sounds and symbols, and hidden forces to direct and control energy, it is one of the most effective tools for achieving your manifested desires, and for programming the mind, and for changing your eocompassing reality. Its magicial power to reprogram the mind causing reality to change is one of the reasons that it is heavily used by corporations, such as religious institutions, banking institutions, and is used by governments and their court system and other government departments, and by other private organizations, especially secret societies.

The empowering knowledge in Word Magic and Symbol Magic that the ruling powers and occult use on humanity, these definitions of words has the potential to unlock many doors of your mind, allowing you to explore a hidden world where you can use words to shape matter, control your destiny, and reprogram your mind. This type of enlightening knowledge of magic and the power of words and symbols are at the core of manifesting reality, furthermore then you will know why using words wisely is important for achieving success and freedom, and restoring your template of your divine human avatar temple, which is your kingdom of God.

Breaking Beyond The Illusionary Simulation

For the people that believe that death does not exist, as in it does not mean the end, because you are not just a body and die, disappear and evaporate. These people discuss the Soul, just as religions discuss the Soul, but the truth is that Soul is that level of consciousness that is recycled through the reincarnation cycle of spiritual development. So if we interperate past the level of the Soul and percieve Spirit, the definition of Spirit is that which is aware that it is all that is, has been, and ever can be, because it is not the body because that's an experience, and its not even Soul that again is an experience. It is eternal Spirit that is connected to all other eternal Spirit, at that level of perceived awareness you know that you are a point of attention within all that is, has been, and ever can be. When we are at that level of awareness, that level of self identity, this means that you are resonating and vibrating at such a high level, that this holographical simulation cannot hold you within its illusionary construct anymore. So we come to then percieve that all the encouragement and pressure when living a life experience in this three dimensional constructed reality, that there is a huge promotion for us to think small and to only identify with the body and its mind, and the falsely constructed labels of the projected limited human life experience. These limitations like its not possible, or I can't, or I'm just tiny me what power do I have, these are the limitations that are holding and trapping people within the holographical simulation. The way you break this hold from the illusionary simulation matrix, is by realizing the true nature of who we truly are, that is the eternal energy of Spirit. Because we are not the mind or body, and we are

not even the Soul ultimately, because
we are Spirit, that is the eternal ultra
violet energetic plasma of Source, from
the Oneness Source field. We are Spirit
of all that is, that has been, and ever
can be, and we are currently having a
manifested physical human experience
in the lower third dimension.
So to wake up consciously to the higher
consciousness fields of Creation, the
key is meditation to be able to stop
your continuious thoughts, and to have
a strict diet of high vibrational foods,
this will give you clarity to percieve the
true realities of life and our
encompassing enviroments, and
beyond in the higher dimensions of the
holographical simulation, and beyond
in the eternal realms.

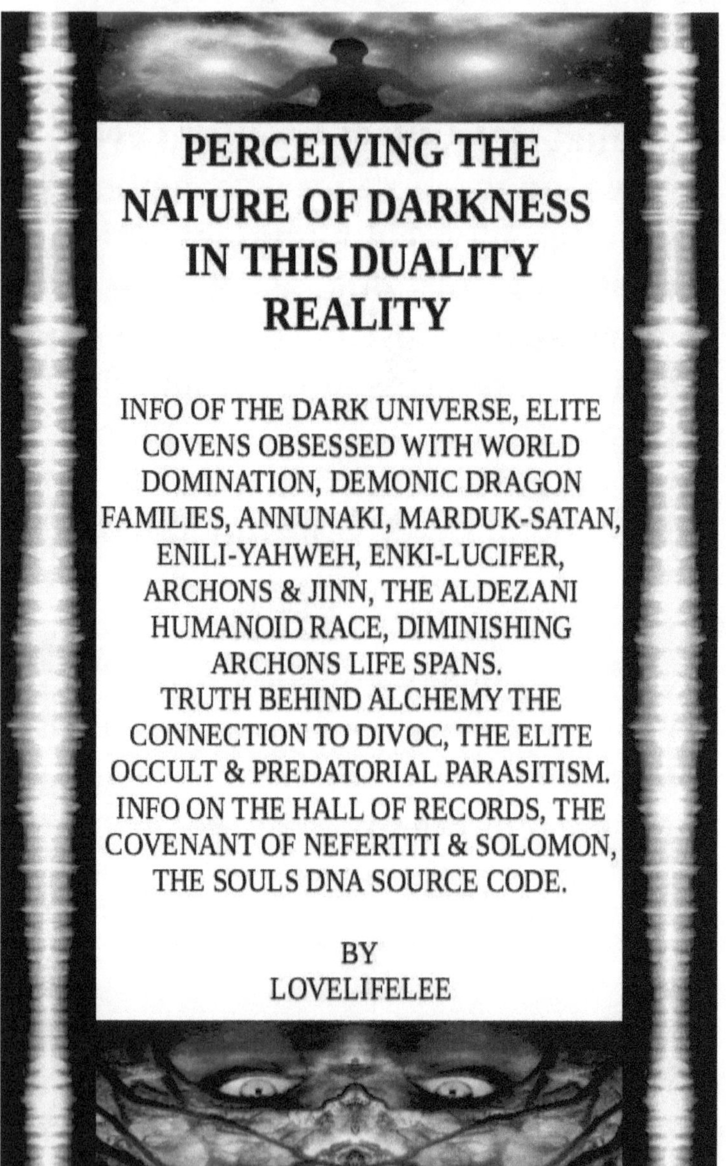
PERCEIVING THE
NATURE OF DARKNESS
IN THIS DUALITY
REALITY

INFO OF THE DARK UNIVERSE, ELITE
COVENS OBSESSED WITH WORLD
DOMINATION, DEMONIC DRAGON
FAMILIES, ANNUNAKI, MARDUK-SATAN,
ENILI-YAHWEH, ENKI-LUCIFER,
ARCHONS & JINN, THE ALDEZANI
HUMANOID RACE, DIMINISHING
ARCHONS LIFE SPANS.
TRUTH BEHIND ALCHEMY THE
CONNECTION TO DIVOC, THE ELITE
OCCULT & PREDATORIAL PARASITISM.
INFO ON THE HALL OF RECORDS, THE
COVENANT OF NEFERTITI & SOLOMON,
THE SOULS DNA SOURCE CODE.

BY
LOVELIFELEE

THE BIOLOGY & CHEMISTRY & MEDICAL FRAUD EXPOSED

& THE TRUTH OF BACTERIA & VIRUSES & ALKALISED HEALING OF THE BIOLOGICAL AVATAR BODY, MEANING THE COLLAPSE OF THE PHARMACEUTICAL INDUSTRY, THE WHOLE MEDICAL BASIS OF TEACHING STANDARD WILL COLLAPSE AS WELL AS

UNIVERSITIES AND EDUCATION SYSTEMS, A NEW/ANCIENT NATURAL WAY TO HEAL, DIET IS KEY TO HAVE WELL BEING TO BE IN FULL HEALTH, TO EVOLVE ASCEND TRANSCEND TO BECOME ILLUMINATED TO ACCESS YOUR ETERNAL LIGHT BODY BY LOVELIFELEE

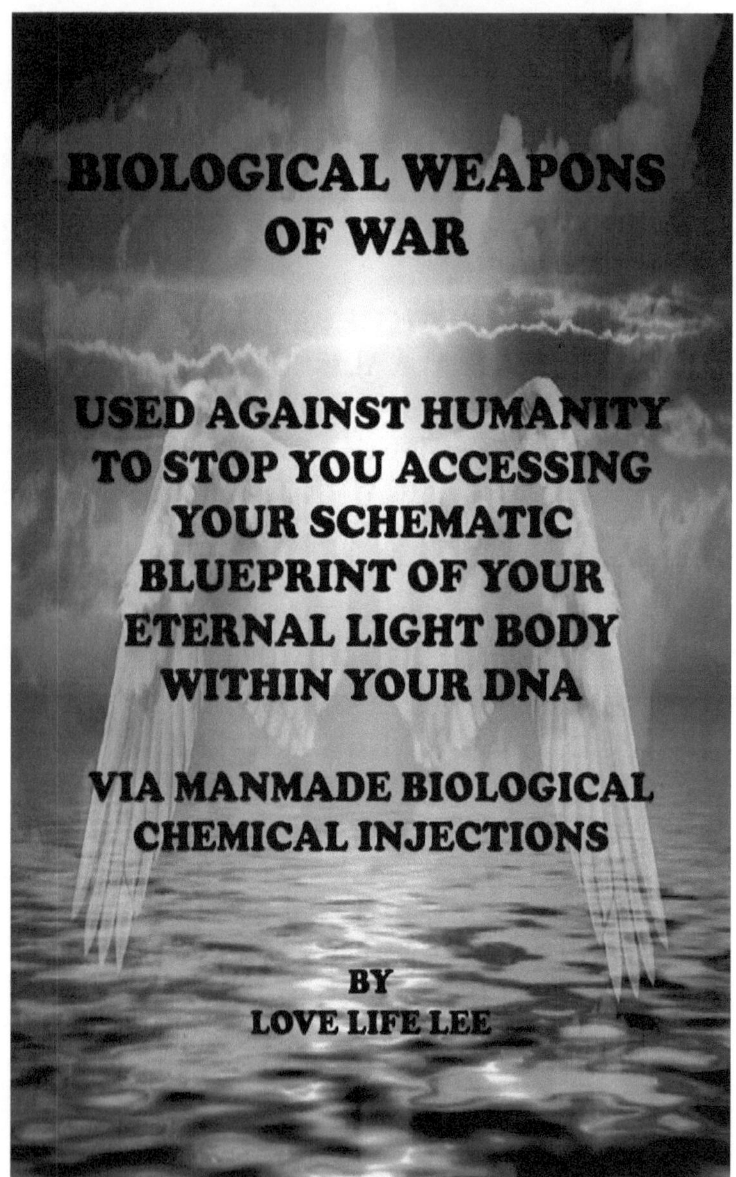
BIOLOGICAL WEAPONS
OF WAR

USED AGAINST HUMANITY
TO STOP YOU ACCESSING
YOUR SCHEMATIC
BLUEPRINT OF YOUR
ETERNAL LIGHT BODY
WITHIN YOUR DNA

VIA MANMADE BIOLOGICAL
CHEMICAL INJECTIONS

BY
LOVE LIFE LEE

The Mental Illness Of GENDER IDENTITY DISORDER

Known As GENDER DYSPHORIA

BY
LOVE LIFE LEE

361

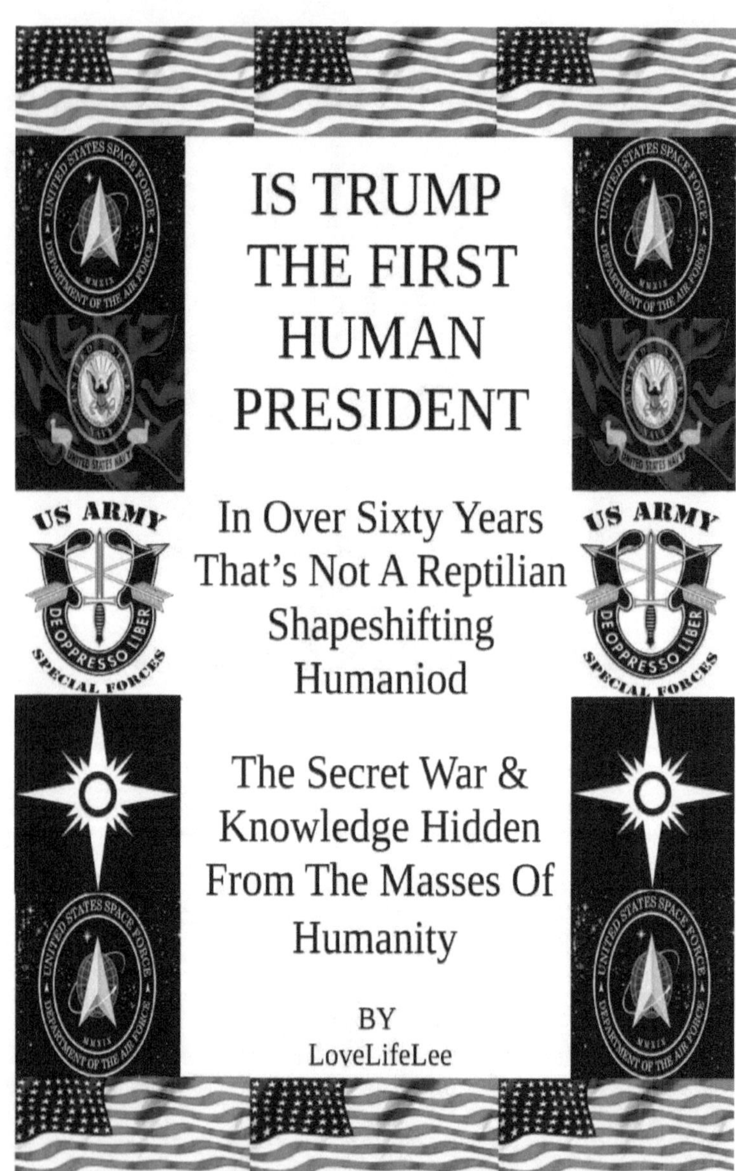
IS TRUMP
THE FIRST
HUMAN
PRESIDENT

In Over Sixty Years
That's Not A Reptilian
Shapeshifting
Humaniod

The Secret War &
Knowledge Hidden
From The Masses Of
Humanity

BY
LoveLifeLee

THE TRUTH OF BIOLOGICAL CHEMICAL WEAPON INJECTIONS

& NASAL INOCULATIONS VIA TESTS
& THE NEW NANO TECHNOLOGIES
BEING INJECTED INTO HUMANITY
TO PURPOSELY MAIM HARM KILL &
REWRITE YOUR DNA ALTERING YOU
TO TRANSHUMANISM WITHOUT
YOUR CONSENT BY THE DISGRACED
FALLEN ANGEL DESCENDANTS
THEIR INTENTION TO HAVE A SMALL
TRANSHUMANISM SLAVE

POPULATION & THEIR MASS
GENOCIDE ON HUMANITY & THE
INGREDIENTS & THE
PERPETRATORS & AUTOIMMUNE
RESPONSES & FUTURE NEURMBURG
TRIALS & AN INTRODUCTION TO
GROW YOUR ETERNAL LIGHT BODY

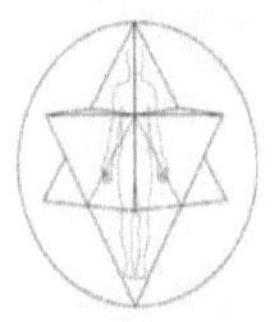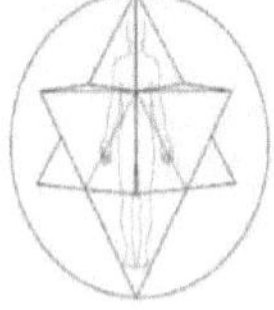

BY
LOVELIFELEE

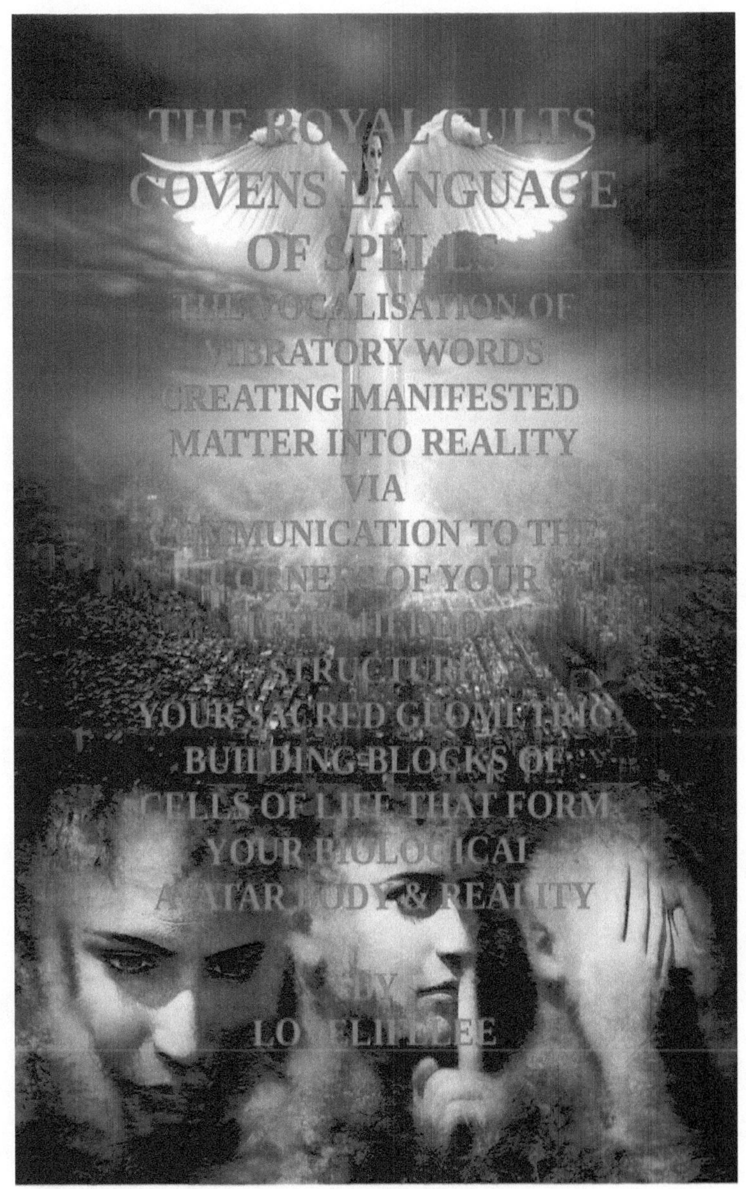
THE ROYAL CULTS
COVENS LANGUAGE
OF SPELLS
THE VOCALISATION OF
VIBRATORY WORDS
CREATING MANIFESTED
MATTER INTO REALITY
VIA
COMMUNICATION TO THE
CORNERS OF YOUR
STRUCTURE
YOUR SACRED GEOMETRIC
BUILDING BLOCKS OF
CELLS OF LIFE THAT FORM
YOUR BIOLOGICAL
AVATAR BODY & REALITY
BY
LOVE LIFE LEE

THE END OF THE THIRD
BANKRUPTCY OF THE
REPUBLIC OF THE UNITED
STATES OF AMERICA & THE
FALL OF QUEEN
ELIZABETH THE SECONDS
REIGN OF SOVEREIGNTY
OF THE U.K. & WORLD
CITIZENS VIA THE COLLAPSE
OF THE BIRTH CERTIFICATE &
CORRUPT LEGAL DOCUMENTS
WORLDWIDE FRAUD & THE
VATICAN COLLAPSE & THE
NEW QUANTUM GRAMMAR
TRUTH SYSTEM INSTALLED
GLOBALLY & THE PATRIOT
THAT SAVED THE REPUBLIC &
SO THE FALL OF GLOBAL
POWER OF THE DISGRACED
ROYAL NON-HUMAN SATANIC
BLOODLINES
BY
LOVELIFELEE

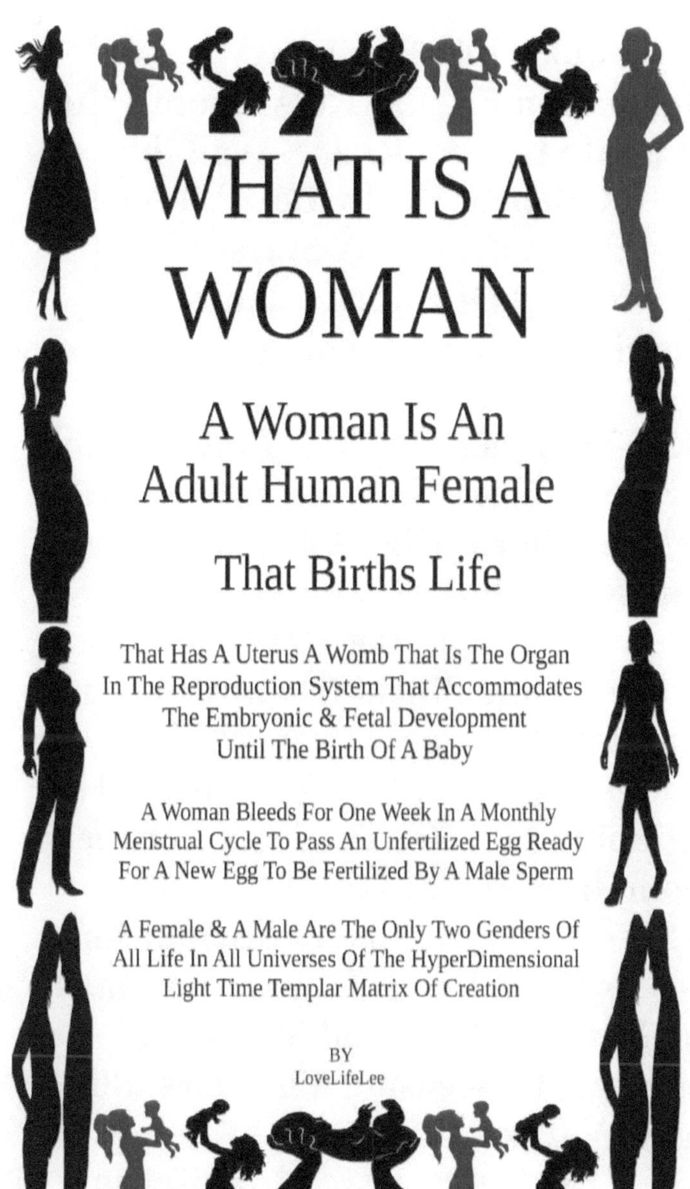

WHAT IS A WOMAN

A Woman Is An Adult Human Female

That Births Life

That Has A Uterus A Womb That Is The Organ
In The Reproduction System That Accommodates
The Embryonic & Fetal Development
Until The Birth Of A Baby

A Woman Bleeds For One Week In A Monthly
Menstrual Cycle To Pass An Unfertilized Egg Ready
For A New Egg To Be Fertilized By A Male Sperm

A Female & A Male Are The Only Two Genders Of
All Life In All Universes Of The HyperDimensional
Light Time Templar Matrix Of Creation

BY
LoveLifeLee

Index Page

Conclusions. Using Energetic Magic Words & Symbols To Raise Your Consciousness & Change Your Envoloping Reality. Breaking Beyond The Illusionary Simulation.

P 358-369 Other books by LoveLifeLee P 370-380 Index Page, Legal Disclaimer, 3 images, Principles of Creation, About this Author, back cover title.

Legal Disclaimer – If you have read any of my thirty four books, you will know I have a wealth of knowledge, with an array of subjects, but my passion has been to pass ancient knowledge & widom about our Eternal Light Body by accessing the Schematic Blueprint within our DNA, to open our Human Angelic Light Body. So I have wrriten books that have discussed the functions of the mind and body, & Chemical reactions & Toxins in the body, and about Psychoactive plants on the mind and body from my own lived experiences and from my knowledge of my Shamanic Practice of the Munay-Ki Nine Rites of initiation. Since a young age I have had the gift of intelligence with a rapid critical thinking mind, and able to critical research in depth, I have no medical qualifications, but from my books you can see I have studied in depth on thousands of subjects. I hope this knowledge is useful and helps anyone suffering from the indoctrination of ideology and philosophy, and Psyop Programming of your Mindset, or anyone who is in conflict with the dark shade of their Ego, or anyone interested in the Mind & Consciousness, or the Hyperdimensional Light Time Templar Matrix of Creation, or in the Eight Principles of Geomancy, of Life, or anyone looking to evolve into their Mer-Ka-Ba Eternal Human Diamond Sun Light Body, or anyone interested in Soul Evolution. Or anyone interested in the truth of reality, or of the many different factions & their agendas of the Secret Wars conducted on humanity, like the Anunnaki & Other groups. Eternal blessings Namaste Love Life Lee. Legal Disclaimer this book is fiction.

The Eight Principles Of Creation

The Eight Principles Of Geomancy Of
Sacred Geometric Animated Life
Manifested By Eternal Spirit Source
Light Beings Consciousness

Principle 1 – The Principle of Mentalism.
Principle 2 – The Principle of
Correspondence.
Principle 3 – The Principle of Vibration.
Principle 4 – The Principle of Polarity.
Principle 5 – The Principle of Rhythum.
Principle 6 – The Principle of Cause &
Effect.
Principle 7 – The Principle of Natural
Law.
Principle 8 – The Generative Principle.

Also interlinked are the Law of Karma,
the Law of Attraction, & Free Will.

About This Author

I was born in a thunder storm of Cosmic dust in the Oneness of all that be. Manifesting in the illusionary University of Light in all its Densities and Vibratory forms, for I the Eternal singular Cell of the Whole Cosmic Consciousness Collective, being connected to all that be in the Creation, the Brahman, the Whole, for we are all One in the Oneness of all that be in the sea of Cosmic Light, a swirling of energy, electromagnetism, the Weak and Strong nuclear forces and Gravity, Divine Eternal Immortal Interdimensional Angelic Light beings of Ultra Violet Energetic Consciousness, creating an avatar a biological Human form body for experience, to come on a mission for the Interdimensional Association of Free Worlds of the Christos Collectives, to pay karma, and manifesting in from the Eternal to raise humanities Collective Consciousness, for Spirit I be for Energy I perceive, all around me multidimensionally this is just how it be you see, frequency vibrating light in wave and powdered form too, opening portholes outside time and space to where we come from, home it be in the Eternal realm of the Kingdoms of Light, allowing humans that have ascended to open their Eternal Light bodies and stopped the cycles of Life and Death, to evolve from Homo-Sapien to Homo-Luminous, we call upon illuminated beings, of Buddha beings, and our Ancestors at this time for transformation to evolve to metamorphosis into the Rainbow Angelic Divine Human Light beings we be in our true nature, we open our Light bodies via our DNA, within are the Schematics of the Blueprint of your Light body and access it we will, and quantum leap ten thousand years into our becoming, allowing us to be fully embodied on this 4th/5th dimensional Earth planet and at the same time we can travel the Stars at instant we will be teleporting to and fro and accessing the Eternal Kingdoms of Light realms, blessed I be for magic I see all around me

in Powdered Light illusionary form,
Divine Spirit it be Gravity, I see Eternal
transcendental Oneness of all that be in
Creation you see blessings Namaste
lovelifelee.

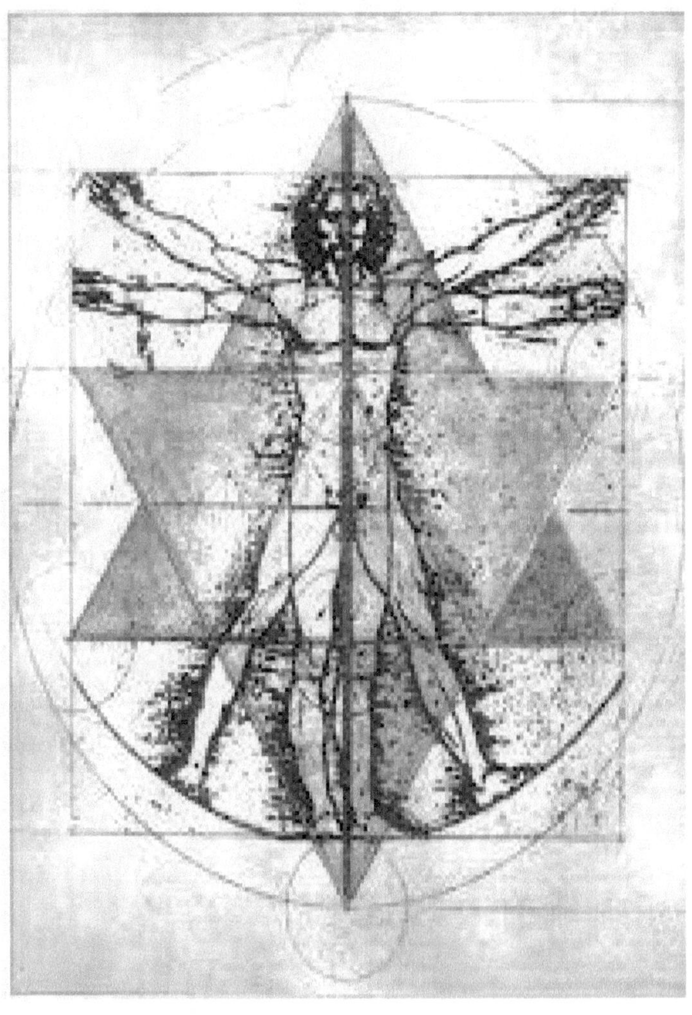

Just Breathe

This book discusses a Star Seeds deciphering of information & Consciousness Awakening on Planet Gaia, an introduction to your Pineal Gland activated by your Kundalini energy system, and how to fully activate your Pineal Gland Chakra Antennas. Also discussed is the Heart the beginning of Life & the link between the Heart & Geometries, & the Scientific Process of Cellular Transmutation of the natural biological Star Gate Passage of Ascension via Celestalline Light Waves. Also discussed is manifesting control of the mind by creating a bridge between the Conscious & Subconscious mind, & the science of the geometric structure of the super advanced biotechnology of DNA & the Blueprint Design of the Angelic Human & its symbiotic relationship to the essence of Spirit & the Merkaba light body. Also discussed is the Psychic childs connection to their Star family & downloaded data they receive, & the evolution cycles of the Soul & humanity.